Things You Need For
The Day Ahead

Protecting Yourself From the Coming Calamities

by

Mark T. Barclay

MARK BARCLAY
PUBLICATIONS

P.O. Box 588 • Midland, Michigan 48640-0588

Things You Need for the Day Ahead
ISBN 978-0-944802-45-8
Copyright © 2009 Mark T. Barclay

Published by Mark Barclay Publications
Mark Barclay Ministries
P.O. Box 588, Midland, MI 48640-0588

Cover by Wake Design Group
info@wakedesigngroup.com

P.O. Box 588 • Midland, Michigan 48640-0588

CONTENTS

ntroduction

I see the worst calamities coming upon the earth in the days ahead, perhaps worse than anything modern mankind has ever known. I see it so clearly when I pray and when I look through the eyes of the prophet's anointing. Even among church people I see pandemic-level events that will drive people out of the power of light into the powers of darkness. Perhaps in all of this is the biblical warning of the great falling away. I don't want to see these things. I don't ask. But I know, without a doubt, they are coming. Anyone who has read even a small portion of the Bible knows that Jesus, as well as the Old Testament prophets, predicted there would be perilous times, famines, earthquakes, wars, and rumors of wars. This cannot be stopped.

At the same time, we know that God will take care of His children—that is, those who serve Him, have given their lives to Him, and follow His ways. We have an extremely convincing witness in our heart and soul that Jesus Christ has not forsaken us and that we are not alone. He knows we are living in the last of the last days, and He has chosen to guide us through them.

I do not want to predict such terrible things. I am an optimist, not a pessimist. However, I would be negligent in my call and derelict in my duties if I did not voice to the body of

Christ what the Lord is saying to me. I do not believe this is a day to be fearful or isolated. It is a day to draw close to God and obey His Word. It is a day to do all that God has called us to do. It is a day to cry out to God and be one of those who walks in His ways.

I know, without a doubt, that the evil onslaught of satan and his demons against God's army is the most treacherous it has ever been. As God's army, we must be the most intense, well-trained soldiers we have ever been, yet all across the land and around the world I see that many are casting off restraint, living sloppier lives, and paying less and less attention to spiritual things. Much of the Church will turn secular in its behavior, practices, and beliefs.

You will watch many preachers fall to worldliness and then fall away. They will claim it is grace or special liberties they have. They will try to teach you that you do not have to obey God or keep the commandments of Jesus Christ. They will fail. They themselves will be deceived. They will walk away from moral lifestyles and become worldly in attitude and behavior. Many will become belligerent and brazen. They will challenge the true prophets of the Lord, and they will lose. Sadly, when they fail, many of their followers will fail with them. In a way, it will be the false prophet (of Baal) against the prophet of God.

There are only two options for life—right and wrong. One either lives morally or immorally. You either live according to the Scriptures, or you don't. There is no in-between. Many will try to convince you otherwise, but they are wrong. We will see many of these messengers fight for sinful, loose lifestyles. Many will be ashamed of the Holy Spirit and will even deny Him. We will actually witness people as they blaspheme the Holy Spirit. This is the unpardonable sin. If you believe in living right and you fight to do so, you will. If you believe in loose living and you fight to do so, you will. This is not difficult to understand.

With the rapid decline of confidence people have in the local church, they are turning to other people and other systems to find spiritual help and advice. These spiritually declining churches are producing practices and performances based on entertainment and celebrity and will attract mass followings. The problem is that they are powerless and carnal. They will even produce some preachers who will be promoted to the level of fame. Man will once again turn to humanism and deception rather than God.

This book is about preparing ourselves for the day ahead, regardless of our level of spirituality, our denomination, or our doctrinal beliefs. All of us will find ourselves in combat and will have to resist evil. Jesus warned that unless the days were shortened, no flesh would be saved (Matt. 24:22).

THE PURPOSE OF THIS BOOK

The Lord has nudged me to help you all I can to be alerted to the time in which you live, to prepare yourself for the journey of a lifetime, to arm yourself so that you can win, and to protect yourself by using the mighty help of our Lord and His biblical systems. Then, as you walk across the earth as a last-days believer, you will not only watch the climax of the ages, but you will be one of those who literally helps climax the ages.

You know that if you're going to plan a camping trip, you must determine what you're going to need. If you're taking the family on vacation, everyone needs to know where they are going and how they are getting there so they can decide how to pack the car or pack for the airplane. If you're going to Alaska in January, you will pack different clothing than for the Bahamas in January. So you must have a plan. What do you need to take with you? And so it is on your spiritual journey. Say that aloud with me, "So it is on my spiritual journey." Christianity is a spiritual journey. It affects every area of your natural life—your money, your family, your mind, and your health. Sure it does—everything. But it is a spiritual journey. Praise God! So on this spiritual journey of walking with God and walking through this life, we must know what it takes. What do we need? What's coming ahead? What should we look for—disaster, despair, victory, conquest, poverty, prosperity—what?

Ten years before he died, as he prepared himself for his final days, I heard my pastor, John Osteen, say, "Lord, what is the plan for John's life? How will I leave the planet? What am I to do during these final days of my life?"

I talked to Roy Hicks Sr., one of my fathers in the faith, and he said something similar before he went to Heaven. He said, "You know, I'm over eighty, teaching the Bible, and pastoring a church I pioneered." (Imagine pioneering a church in your eighties!) He said, "I'm traveling, teaching, and helping preachers, but I just keep asking the Lord what His plan is for my final days."

I had a conversation with Dr. George Evans from San Diego, another one of my fathers and leaders in the faith. He is now also in his eighties, and it's the same for him. He said, "I was talking to the Lord about my final days. I don't plan to die tomorrow or next week, but I've got to have a plan. I need a plan. What do I need to do while I still have these next few years to make an impact on the body of Christ?"

Let me help you—it's not just the older folks who need to pay attention to life. Young people need to also. Just because you're not older doesn't mean you can take for granted that everything's going to be okay for you. Many people are going home to Heaven early. It's shocking to many of us how quickly Heaven is filling up and how fast the earth is emptying. Everyone has to be ready. If we live tomorrow and the next day (which is our confession, of course) and next month and next year and ten years from now and the Lord doesn't return, what are we going to need? What's the plan? I can come up with ten things we are going to need as Christians and Christian leaders for both our personal lives and for our ministries—ten things we're going to need for the day ahead.

Almost everything around us is trying to stop us from being a productive, active Christian. I'll tell you what's going to separate us from the troubled people of the world—our God and Him delivering us from the lions' den and the fiery furnace. There are going to be some lions' dens. There are going to be some fiery furnaces. There's going to be some stuff to deal with. You're going to have to battle off some sickness and disease. There are going to be some times you're flowing in money and some times you're not. Listen to me! No matter what is yelling at you—lions' den, fiery furnace, or bankruptcy—God is able to deliver us out of it all, and that's what's going to separate us from others in the day ahead. Our God is going to come through for us.

May God use this book to not only alert you to coming events but to help you escape all these things that will come down upon the earth between now and the day you stand before the Son of the Living God.

Dangers to Come

Before I go any further, I want to tell you that I plan to show you what to do (or at least what you will need) for the day ahead. I certainly don't intend to discourage you or to write a fear-based book. I want to help you, and I want to help fortify you for what's coming.

THE DANGERS TO COME

There is no doubt about it—danger is upon us. Around every corner of life lurks something or someone who wants to hurt us or even annihilate us. I don't exaggerate this, yet I am not afraid of it. As last-days Christians, we must understand the day in which we live and live according to the Word of God—a life of faith, a life in the Word, and a life of being led by the Holy Spirit, without fear and compromise. It is a day that darkness has come upon the human race in disproportionate, quantum levels. We don't have to become a victim to it. As a matter fact, we are instructed by the Bible to not only survive but to overcome.

These days are, without a doubt, the "last days." Over 2000 years ago, on the Jewish holiday of Pentecost, the Lord poured out of His Spirit in that upper room filled with hungry believers. Peter was there and experienced that great initial outpouring. His answer to a critical crowd of onlookers and skeptics was recorded.

Acts 2:15-17

For these are not drunken, as ye suppose, seeing it is but the third hour of the day. But this is that which was spoken by the prophet Joel; And it shall come to pass <u>in the last days,</u> saith God, I will pour out of my Spirit upon all flesh . . .

If the early believers knew that the day of Pentecost was the last days and God confirmed it, then we are certainly living in the "last" of the last days now. You do not need a prophet to reveal this to you. I am simply bringing it to your attention so that as you read through this book, you will more and more realize the need for its content.

The prophets of old saw both the good and the bad. The prophets of today are similar, considering they don't hold the identical position description. I flow in this anointing and gift and when I see things, I see both the things that make people happy and the things that are sad. I wish I didn't. I wish God would only show me pretty things and things that bring joy. I know why He doesn't. He wants us to be blessed and safe, not just soulfully and emotionally soothed. He wants to warn us of the dangers ahead. Any loving parent will shout warnings to their child if danger is present or great harm is imminent.

Though I am a strong optimist, at times I must look at the opposite arena of life and see what is going on. In these last few years it has been blatantly evident that things are deteriorating rapidly. Sin is at an all-time high because Christians are dramatically letting their guard down. Crime is at an all-time high because society as a whole is deteriorating rapidly. Jesus predicted wars, rumors of wars, and other calamities.

Matthew 24:6-7

And ye shall hear of wars and rumours of wars: see that ye be not troubled: for all these things must come to pass, but the end is not yet. For nation shall rise against nation, and kingdom against kingdom: and there shall be famines, and pestilences, and earthquakes, in divers places.

The great Apostle Paul also predicted perilous times:

2 Timothy 3:1

This know also, that in the last days perilous times shall come.

Read the rest of this great chapter of the Bible and see the warnings, time and again, about humans and their terrible ways.

The Prophet Isaiah warned us about this filthy onslaught that would constantly cause the decay of morals and some of the nastiest behavior man has ever known.

Isaiah 60:2

For, behold, the darkness shall cover the earth, and gross darkness the people . . .

I feel called to warn God's people about these traps and perils. I know deep on the inside of me that God has anointed me to prepare His people for His coming. I have realized this since the day I was called to preach. I know that God has called me to be a prophetic voice to the last generations before He climaxes the ages.

Jesus warned us that the day of His coming would be just like the day of Noah and the day of Lot. In those days, people were marrying, building, buying, and selling, and they were living as if there were no God and no judgment coming. Boy, did they find out the hard way! It seems as though many people today fit this description perfectly. I take it as a sign that His coming is at hand, just like He predicted. We must not only survive but conquer the times and be ready for His appearing.

We are not alone! There is no way the Lord Jesus would leave us to ourselves. No way! No way would He expect us to go through this life (which is like a minefield in a combat zone) without His guidance. No way would God allow us to be devoured by His adversary or our enemies. No, my brother and sister, He is right here with us, doing everything in His power to protect us and keep us strong, holy, and spiritual.

When I was in Bible school, many years ago now, an elderly preacher pulled me aside and told me things to come. He said, "I see people in an airport, looking at things like television sets hanging from the ceiling, and as people wait for their flight departures, they watch the news." He saw people getting on planes and then leaving them because the Holy Spirit led them not to fly on that flight. They disembarked and then watched their plane blow up or crash. He saw God's people going into restaurants and the Holy Spirit telling them to leave, even though they had already ordered. They obeyed God and didn't even get a block or two away when the entire contents of the restaurant blew out into the street from an explosion.

Today we commonly hear about these terrible terrorist activities. He did not. Through this elderly preacher, I received the commission to warn God's people about things to come and help them prepare.

Time of Calamity

I predict the worst time of calamity that church people have ever known. I don't want to predict this, but I can't help what I see by the Spirit. Many of our largest, fastest-growing churches in America are teaching our people to avoid or stay away from the very things that make them strong and lethal to evil. For example, the Bible teaches us that faith is the victory that overcomes this world. Faith comes by hearing the Word of God preached, yet many churches have cut back on the preaching and have even replaced it with other things. The Bible also teaches us that praying in our prayer language builds us up in our most holy faith, but these same churches teach people to avoid praying in our heavenly language. These and many more things like them are weakening us in a day when we need more power and more faith to overcome the darkness. Certainly this is not a day when we need less. Though many choose not to hold God's hand as they walk through life, you do it anyway.

So, seeing that we are surrounded by these things and knowing that God has not left us alone, I write this book so you can get your family in line with His Word and be ready for the sound of the trumpet.

PERILOUS TIMES

2 Timothy 3:1

This know also, that in the last days perilous times shall come.

Look at the next verses:

2 Timothy 3:2

For men shall be lovers of their own selves, covetous, boasters, proud, blasphemers, disobedient to parents, unthankful, unholy . . .

2 Timothy 3:3

Without natural affection, trucebreakers, false accusers, incontinent, fierce, despisers of those that are good . . .

2 Timothy 3:4

Traitors, heady, highminded, lovers of pleasures more than lovers of God . . .

2 Timothy 3:5

Having a form of godliness, but denying the power thereof: from such turn away.

2 Timothy 3:6

For of this sort are they which creep into houses, and lead captive silly women laden with sins, led away with divers lusts . . .

2 Timothy 3:7

Ever learning, and never able to come to the knowledge of the truth.

2 Timothy 3:8

Now as Jannes and Jambres withstood Moses, so do these also resist the truth: men of corrupt minds, reprobate concerning the faith.

2 Timothy 3:9

But they shall proceed no further: for their folly shall be manifest unto all men, as their's also was.

I want to point out the second verse to you. This verse holds the key phrase to interpreting our end times. It clearly says that ". . . men shall be . . ." If your mind is set only on earth-quakes and famine and wars and rumors of wars, you may be missing the heart of what the Lord is saying to us today.

There is no doubt that humans are among their own worst enemies. I am personally appalled at what is going on, even in the great United States of America. I hate the murders, rapes, and abductions. I really hate the molestation and murder of our young. It is outrageous that most of America is not outraged! What about the terrorists? Most of them function in the name of their god and religion. Pedophiles? Experts say they are usually someone we know and trust, or even worse, a relative. Outrageous!

I just don't believe we have to fall prey to all of this. We can and should fight it. It is the will of God that we do something about it. It is the will of God that we fight it. In the following chapters, I will show you what to do to withstand and resist this evil.

DECEPTION

2 Thessalonians 2:3

Let no man deceive you by any means: for that day shall not come, except there come a falling away first, and that man of sin be revealed, the son of perdition . . .

Let's dissect this scripture a little and see what it reveals to us about the day in which we live.

Let No Man Deceive You

Here we are again being told to watch out for humans who could deceive us. This is actually a dual warning. First, watch out for that person or group of people who could deceive you. Second, watch out for deception itself. These wrong voices and deceiving powers are two of our greatest perils of last-days living. Jesus said so.

By Any Means

This means any way or avenue that deception can get to you. I sadly include much of the preaching of the day. It is watered down, and a lot of it is heresy. These seducing spirits are causing people to leave the faith and start practicing the ways of the world all over again. A lot of loose living and pretending is done in the name of church and Christianity. Many people totally disobey the Bible and say that the Lord told them it is okay. Many of them actually learned sin while attending church and also by fellowshipping with those who still commit sin. This is a lethal practice. "Any means" would include every way, and that includes things done and said by preachers who change the Word when they preach.

Except There Come a Falling Away

All of my Christian life I have heard about this great falling away. Of course, the Bible also tells us about this. There are warnings to all Christians that they should fight and repel the elements that lead to apostasy. Apostasy doesn't always mean the blasphemy of the Holy Spirit. In order to "fall away" one must first begin "falling away." Many Christians today seem to be growing lukewarm and living worldly without any conviction.

Man of Sin Revealed

We are in the era of the antichrist. You can feel the antichrist in the air. Pre-antichrist demons are now working among humans and even trying to get into the churches. They have the assignment to prep the world for the antichrist to take over. They will mesmerize the sinner and even deceive many Christians.

FALSE REVIVALS AND FAMILIAR SPIRITS

Jesus absolutely warned us about false revivals. I see this happening already. I am also witnessing so-called revivals that function partially by the Holy Ghost and partially by familiar spirits.

Matthew 24:4–5

And Jesus answered and said unto them, Take heed that no man deceive you. For many shall come in my name, saying, I am Christ; and shall deceive many.

These verses make more sense when you understand the definition of the word "Christ." Yes, it refers to "Jesus, the Christ" and is actually defined as "the Anointed One and His anointing." I truly believe that Jesus was warning us to watch out for not only those who claim to be the new Christ but also those who claim they are the anointed ones.

I have noticed during the past few years that whenever a group of believers has a special meeting with manifestations, they want to market it or advertise it as "the" place where God is moving. In fact, some say it is the only place where God is moving and that we all should go there to see it and even capture it to bring it home. I am not against revival, signs, wonders, and manifestations, as long as they are of the "Holy" Spirit. It never sets well with me, though, when they are advertised as being the only place on earth. The other problem is when they say it is the beginning of the next move of God, and if we want to be in the next move of God we should get to that location immediately. I am sad to report that so far this has not been the case at all, even though many people, including preachers, have traveled from around the world to these revivals.

What is even more alarming to me is the fact that, in many of these meetings, the ministers seem to flow partially with the Holy Spirit and partially with a familiar spirit. I have witnessed that even seducing spirits are sometimes free to manifest at will. God help us!

We must be open to God's future outpourings and visitations, but we must also beware lest we be easily deceived. As the day of the Lord approaches, I predict that we will have false revivals—those "manifestation" meetings where God does not even show up at all. They will have more of a New Age spiritism and mysticism atmosphere, where New Age doctrines and practices will be used regularly. I also see that these "outpourings" will be greater in number, more widely advertised to the nations, and occur on a more frequent basis. I also predict that these will be more the work of the pre-antichrist spirits than the work of the Holy Ghost. The confusing part for many Christians will be the fact that in the midst of all this, Jesus will be doing His work as well, and there will be genuine outpourings and visitations.

Check out these verses:

Matthew 7:21–23

Not every one that saith unto me, Lord, Lord, shall enter into the kingdom of heaven; but he that doeth the will of my Father which is in heaven. Many will say to me in that day, Lord, Lord, have we not prophesied in thy name? and in thy name have cast out devils? and in thy name done many wonderful works? And then will I profess unto them, I never knew you: depart from me, ye that work iniquity.

EARTH DANGERS

Luke 21:10

Then said he unto them, Nation shall rise against nation, and kingdom against kingdom . . .

Luke 21:11

And great earthquakes shall be in divers places, and famines, and pestilences; and fearful sights and great signs shall there be from heaven.

We certainly have seen this come to manifestation. We have seen entire cities destroyed by hurricanes, and then earthquakes, and then tsunamis. Forest fires have burned whole counties, and tempestuous-level winds have ripped apart cities. It is interesting how the news reports terrible drought on one continent and extreme rainfall with damaging flooding on another (both causing unbearable conditions, deadly to the human race and animals) or one people freezing to death, while others fall to the ground from heat exhaustion.

WARS AND RUMORS OF WARS

All of my life I have heard of wars going on somewhere in the world, some far away and some close to home. Since I have been able to read, I have seen the reports of what war does to its victims. I was born in war, meaning that my country, the United States of America, was at war with Korea when I came into this world. It wasn't over long when the Vietnam war escalated, and I was called upon as a U.S. Marine to fight. Then small wars broke out here and there, all over the globe. I think of Kuwait and then the retaliation of 911 in Afghanistan. Soon after that, we went to war in Iraq. This all happened in a few short years. Only God knows where it will happen next.

TERRORISM

Terrorists are most people's main concern. For many years we have watched the news report to us the dastardly deeds of these cowardly attackers who are more than willing to blow themselves up in order to murder even the innocent. They use unconventional warfare tactics, and they attack civilians instead of military targets. Actually, these are not even warfare tactics, as you know if you are a military man. They are acts of murder and hatred. There is just something terribly wrong with stepping on a bus and blowing up a bunch of kids.

Most people now live in fear, including here in the U.S. Many want to believe that terrorism is just going to go away, that it is a phase we are going through, or it is just a season that will eventually pass all on its own. But I tell you differently. Even when we win the war on terror, there will still be plenty of evil people to attack and harm your life and try to break through your parameters of safety and security. We need to come to the realization that terrorists are not only a group of radical Muslims or an out-of-control, civilian army working in the shadows. Terrorism can also be a person stalking you or randomly selecting someone to terrorize or torture.

DISEASE

Perhaps our biggest challenges and enemies of the last days are going to be bacteria, viral infections, and diseases. Not to keep dwelling on negatives, but this is already at a crisis level globally. It will take the absolute intervention of God to give us the disinfectants and effective antidotes to deal with this massive attack. I am talking about an intervention by God, not just what we can do in the natural with sanitation and hygiene. It has been many years since any real cure has been discovered for known diseases that kill by the thousands. We desperately need God on this scene of our lives. Ultimately, neither man nor satan is in charge. In the end, God will have His way.

NATURAL DISASTERS

We can no longer say that bad things are coming—they are here! For many years we have said that in the end times natural disasters and weird weather patterns would be coming. They are now here. From tsunamis to earthquakes to floods to hurricanes, things are ferocious. Every other day we hear of another natural disaster somewhere. Every other week or so, something takes many lives (or at least it seems this way). The end is upon us and, like it or not, we are the last-days people. We are perhaps the last generation of humans to live on the planet. We are surely living in the end times, and all evidence supports this.

DEMONS

Demons are ferocious, and they have zero compassion on humans. They are deadly, but they would actually rather pervert you and parade you before our God as a traitor and a deserter than kill you. If they kill you, they lose because you go to Heaven—the ultimate victory. Demons are real, and they must be dealt with. They must be addressed. They just cannot be permitted to have free access into our lives, to come and go as they wish. I will cover this more in Chapter 3.

I have noticed these past few years that we have little (if any) teaching on how to deal with these evil, invisible enemy soldiers. It seems that the body of Christ went way overboard in dealing with them and even got into false doctrines and weird practices, but now we have overcorrected.

THERE ARE THINGS WE CAN DO

There are several scriptural things we can do to protect ourselves, all by the design of God. I have said many times in my preaching and will mention more than once in this writing that God does not expect us to walk through these dark times by ourselves. It is God's will that we walk with Him and that He guides us through these days and even through the valley of the shadow of death. No matter what comes down upon the earth or how bad things get, the Lord Jesus will bring us through and deliver us. This is His Word. It is the Bible. Count on it!

Chapter 2 — Warning #2

Escaping the Danger

I keep telling myself and all those who hear me that we are not alone. God is with us. There is no way that He will allow us to move forward without Him and His protection. There is no way we will walk out these last days without the Spirit of the Lord guiding us.

Luke 21:36

Watch ye therefore, and pray always, that ye may be accounted worthy to escape all these things that shall come to pass, and to stand before the Son of man.

Luke 21:36 NLT

Keep alert at all times. And pray that you might be strong enough to escape these coming horrors and stand before the Son of Man.

Let's take a better look at these verses and the insights they hold for us. First of all, they tell us to pray always. This doesn't mean to do nothing but pray. No one could do that and still raise a family and hold a job. A young preacher asked me how long I pray. I told him that I don't necessarily pray for really long periods of time, but I don't let much time go by without praying. In fact, one of my men told me once that I will be sitting with him or in the car with him, and I'll just take off praying in the spirit or talking to God as if He and I were already in a conversation (and actually we were). We should never be out of touch with Heaven. Constantly throughout the day we should be talking to the Father. Also, of course, we know to pray with fervency and lock into the place of prayer until we are satisfied in our soul that we have prayed things through and heard from God.

This verse also teaches us that we should be people of prayer. If we stay in prayer, we will most likely stay out of sin. If we stay in prayer, we will most likely stay out of the world and keep the world out of us. Prayer itself requires God's attention, and therefore it is difficult to have God's attention and remain in His presence and still want the world. We have learned also that God guides us through prayer times, thus He vectors us away from dangers.

This same verse in the New Living Translation tells us that when we pray, it makes us strong. When we pray, we endure and we overcome. If we live a life of prayer, we will be strong enough to overcome this world and the crud that is coming down upon the human race.

So ... don't let anything hinder your prayer life!

PLAN TO ESCAPE

I plan to escape all these things. No, I do not fit the description of some who say I have an escapist mentality. No, I do not. I am not a defeatist, and I do not believe we will all be beat up and defeated and that the Lord will have to come quickly or none of us will make it. I believe quite the opposite.

I believe there will be those of us who will overcome, and we will see victory over all these things that are coming down upon the earth. We will be ready for the Lord's appearing. That's the whole point. Heaven expects us to prepare ourselves and be spiritually fit. We are overcomers, and not just with words alone.

The previous verse began with a warning to watch. It said to look up and watch for His coming. I like to say, "Watch your mouth, watch your attitude, watch your lifestyle."

Hebrews 2:3

How shall we escape, if we neglect so great salvation; which at the first began to be spoken by the Lord, and was confirmed unto us by them that heard him . . .

There is no doubt that the Lord is telling us to pay attention to our walk. If we live in negligence, we will not have what it takes to escape the evil and the snares of the evil one. However, if we do pay attention to our Christian walk and purpose to be spiritual, we will be powerful.

This verse deals with negligence. It is a warning to every one of us to do our part. So many modern Christians want it all to be on God. They just don't like the feeling that it isn't all in the hands of God. We must be responsible to do our part. There are many verses to support this.

We know that it takes all of God's work in our life to be a winner. We know that Jesus' grace is sufficient for us. It is sufficient to help us get through tough things and to deal with the elements.

Hebrews 12:25

See that ye refuse not him that speaketh. For if they escaped not who refused him that spake on earth, much more shall not we escape, if we turn away from him that speaketh from heaven . . .

This verse is crucial to last-days survival. Many will not make it. Many will turn away. Many will be defeated, and in their defeat they will blame God (or at least wonder where He is). I'm seeing so many churches turning away from the Holy Spirit. It's the voice of the Spirit that will guide us through the minefield. If we turn our ear away from Him, who will guide us? If we listen to the voice from Heaven (the Holy Spirit) and follow that voice, He will help us. If we don't, He won't. So, as the verse just said, ". . . refuse not him that speaketh."

Jude 1:20

But ye, beloved, building up yourselves on your most holy faith, praying in the Holy Ghost . . .

I asked all five of my fathers in the faith (Drs. John Osteen, Lester Sumrall, Hilton Sutton, George Evans, and Roy Hicks Sr.) what they thought was the missing link or the thing that is causing people to be weak and so easily defeated. Each of them answered in a similar way: "Believers won't even spend fifteen minutes a day praying in the spirit to build themselves up in their most holy faith."

The Bible is clear about what to do, but it seems that few actually do it. The Bible explicitly predicts danger and evil times, yet so many modern Christians do not seem to take those warnings to heart. This is the greatest of all calamities. It reminds me of Noah's day. No one really took his warning to heart until it was too late. Don't let this be you, my friend.

GOD MAKES A WAY OF ESCAPE

1 Corinthians 10:13

There hath no temptation taken you but such as is common to man: but God is faithful, who will not suffer you to be tempted above that ye are able; but will with the temptation also make a way to escape, that ye may be able to bear it.

As we take a closer look at this verse, we learn a couple of encouraging things. God has spoken. He said that no temptation has taken you but such as is common to man. That's right, not common to satan or demons but common to man. This absolutely levels the playing field, and it limits the evil one. The devil must find a way to tempt us in the human realm. Man, I like this! This is God setting up the battle for us. He is projecting the victory for us.

Secondly, God tells us that He will not allow us to be tempted above what we can bear. This encourages me. Not only does it tell us that God is going to stop the tempter at some point but that He believes in us and knows we can endure.

What about this next encouraging point—God said to us that He will make a way of escape. Man, I like that too. No matter what tempts us, He will show us the way out. We do not have to fall for it. We do not have to do it. Being tempted is not a sin. Following that temptation to its fruition and acting upon temptation is sin. You "fall" into temptation, but you "commit" sin. We can beat the elements of the day if we will just follow the Lord's way and live His lifestyle.

LED BY THE SPIRIT

John 16:13

Howbeit when he, the Spirit of truth, is come, he will guide you into all truth: for he shall not speak of himself; but whatsoever he shall hear, that shall he speak: and he will shew you things to come.

I love this verse, and I love the meaning of it. I am convinced that the Holy Spirit is with us and though life is like a minefield, He will tell us exactly how and where to step. That's the beauty of His presence in our lives. It's the benefit of being a Spirit-filled Christian.

I thank the Lord every day that I am Spirit-filled, and I enjoy Him in my private life and His total input on raising my children and building His ministry. I wish that all people everywhere were born-again, Spirit-filled Christians. What a privilege it has been to have Him in our home and in our lives.

GIVING AND SAFETY ARE MARRIED

I will guarantee you that most Christians have never considered what I am about to show you. I do not mean that in any arrogant way but rather that it just hasn't been taught this way very often. God wants us to live a safe life, protected from evil. This whole book is about living in the last days and beating the evil of the day. That's what I am dealing with again as we open these next three passages of scripture.

God promises protection through the tithe. Now, don't flip the page just because I am talking for a moment about the tithe!

Malachi 3:8-12

Will a man rob God? Yet ye have robbed me. But ye say, Wherein have we robbed thee? In tithes and offerings. Ye are cursed with a curse: for ye have robbed me, even this whole nation. Bring ye all the tithes into the storehouse, that there may be meat in mine house, and prove me now herewith, saith the LORD of hosts, if I will not open you the windows of heaven, and pour you out a blessing, that there shall not be room enough to receive it. And I will rebuke the devourer for your sakes, and he shall not destroy the fruits of your ground; neither shall your vine cast her fruit before the time in the field, saith the LORD of hosts. And all nations shall call you blessed: for ye shall be a delightsome land, saith the LORD of hosts.

He will rebuke the devourer for your sake. There is no more powerful promise of protection than this one right here. There is not a more powerful promise of God's intervention in the time of trouble than this one right here. God Himself is on the scene of your life, actually forcing the enemy to pull back. Wow! And some people think tithing is ridiculous. How silly of them.

This following verse reveals another encouraging truth to us. We learn by it that our giving is in direct relationship with our future and the evil that lies ahead of us. This verse gives us the connotation that our giving is what gives us the power over that evil. We all hope and pray for nothing but the best, yet the enemy keeps setting snares and traps for us. We do not always see it, but God knows it. Our giving to His work is one of the insurance programs the kingdom of God offers that helps us overcome these dangers.

Ecclesiastes 11:2

Give a portion to seven, and also to eight; for thou knowest not what evil shall be upon the earth.

As you read this verse from Galatians, you will have to surrender any thoughts you may have that your giving and bad happenings aren't connected. It is quite simple, actually. If you sow to your flesh, you will reap corruption. If you sow to your flesh, you will reap from the system of the flesh. I do not plan to reap any corruption in my life. Many corrupt their entire families because their sowing is not biblical. I plan to have no corrupt mind, no corrupt mouth, no corrupt wife, no corrupt ministries, no corrupt children, etc. I refuse this corruption every time I sow to the Spirit, instead of my own flesh.

If you sow to the Spirit, you will reap life. The only way to sow to the Spirit is to sow to the **work** of the Spirit. You cannot hand off your tithes and offerings to the person of the Holy Spirit, even though we know He is present in our church services. You cannot send your money to Heaven. I sometimes tease my home church and tell them that I don't have a vacuum tube in the ushers' room, like the drive-up window at the bank, whereby I send their tithes to Heaven. The only way to sow their money to the Spirit is to sow it into the work of the Spirit.

Galatians 6:8

For he that soweth to his flesh shall of the flesh reap corruption; but he that soweth to the Spirit shall of the Spirit reap life everlasting.

ABSTAIN FROM APPEARANCES OF EVIL

This is one of the most powerful means of protection the Lord Jesus gave us. It is actually very simple to understand. Abstain from all appearances of evil. If you avoid and abstain from all "appearances" of evil, you will most likely be out of the reach of evil. When we pay attention to this level of evil, we blockade the deeper, more damaging levels of evil.

The "appearance" of evil is the first level. If others don't see my car in the bar parking lot (because I'm not there), I have escaped the danger and evil that is in the bar. Do you understand? If I am concerned about what it "looks" like, I surely won't involve myself in any deeper level of danger, evil, or wrongdoing.

The word "abstain" means to hold oneself back. Crime is normally related to crime, and sin is normally related to sin. In other words, if you are not selling drugs or taking drugs, you won't be there when the drug war explodes or the drug bust goes down. If your car is never at the bar (because you are avoiding even the "appearance" of drinking), you will not be exposed to or tempted by any evil or dangerous situations at the bar, neither will you be tempted to drink. It's pretty simple, and it's the reason the Lord wants us to avoid these appearances.

Abstaining from the very appearance of evil is one of the simplest yet most powerful actions you can take. I have always wondered why Christians want to look like the world and act like the world. Many seem to have the desire to imitate or identify with the sinner. This is a form of betrayal to Christ who died for you, and it has the potential to bring you great harm.

THE WORDS OF YOUR MOUTH

The Bible is the guide to good living and the navigation system for the last-days believer. It is the absolute, infallible Word of the Living God. The Bible says that life and death are in the power of the tongue. It also teaches us that we can have what we say (Prov. 18:21, Mark 11:23–24). For years I heard the critics say that Kenneth E. Hagin made up this doctrine or that he and Kenneth Copeland and Charles Capps taught it out of context. I could see it in the Scriptures, and I knew these critics were wrong. If it is in the Book, it's okay to believe it. If the Bible teaches it, we can walk it out. We can live it.

Our mouth may be one of the best weapons we have. It can literally launch the Word of God against the enemy. It can encourage us and build up those around us. The Word says to allow no corrupt communication to come out of our mouth (Eph. 4:29). There are many verses that refer to the fruit of our lips—too many to ignore. Bible people are going to use their mouth properly and scripturally. We will find ourselves dealing with evil, just as Jesus dealt with the devil during temptation.

PSALM 91 PROTECTION

Psalm 91

He that dwelleth in the secret place of the most High shall abide under the shadow of the Almighty. I will say of the LORD, He is my refuge and my fortress: my God; in him will I trust. Surely he shall deliver thee from the snare of the fowler, and from the noisome pestilence. He shall cover thee with his feathers, and under his wings shalt thou trust: his truth shall be thy shield and buckler. Thou shalt not be afraid for the terror by night; nor for the arrow that flieth by day; Nor for the pestilence that walketh in darkness; nor for the destruction that wasteth at noonday. A thousand shall fall at thy side, and ten thousand at thy right hand; but it shall not come nigh thee. Only with thine eyes shalt thou behold and see the reward of the wicked. Because thou hast made the LORD, which is my refuge, even the most High, thy habitation; There shall no evil befall thee, neither shall any plague come nigh thy dwelling. For he shall give his angels charge over thee, to keep thee in all thy ways. They shall bear thee up in their hands, lest thou dash thy foot against a stone. Thou shalt tread upon the lion and adder: the young lion and the dragon shalt thou trample under feet. Because he hath set his love upon me, therefore will I deliver him: I will set him on high, because he hath known my name. He shall call upon me, and I will answer him: I will be with him in trouble; I will deliver him, and honour him. With long life will I satisfy him, and shew him my salvation.

MY CONFESSION AND BENEDICTION

I have spoken this over our congregation every time I minister the Word for the past twenty-five years. It has become the official benediction of Living Word International Church. May it bless you today.

I confess Psalm 91 over you, right now, in Jesus' name. I say that no evil shall befall you, and no plague shall come nigh your dwelling, for He has given His angels charge over you to keep you in all your ways. I say that no drugged or drunk driver, no rapist, no burglar, no murderer, no suicide, no terrorist, no evil spirit, no evil person, no sickness, no disease, no fire, no flood, no crash . . . none of these evil things shall come near you or your immediate loved ones. You are going to live in great peace, great joy, great prosperity, and great safety and be a powerful witness for Him, in Jesus' name!

A FEW OF MY FAVORITE VERSES

Psalm 34:17

The righteous cry, and the LORD heareth, and delivereth them out of all their troubles.

Psalm 46:1

God is our refuge and strength, a very present help in trouble.

Matthew 6:13

And lead us not into temptation, but deliver us from evil: For thine is the kingdom, and the power, and the glory, forever. Amen.

2 Corinthians 10:4–5

(For the weapons of our warfare are not carnal, but mighty through God to the pulling down of strong holds;) Casting down imaginations, and every high thing that exalteth itself against the knowledge of God, and bringing into captivity every thought to the obedience of Christ . . .

Deuteronomy 28:1-14

And it shall come to pass, if thou shalt hearken diligently unto the voice of the LORD thy God, to observe and to do all his commandments which I command thee this day, that the LORD thy God will set thee on high above all nations of the earth: And all these blessings shall come on thee, and overtake thee, if thou shalt hearken unto the voice of the LORD thy God. Blessed shalt thou be in the city, and blessed shalt thou be in the field. Blessed shall be the fruit of thy body, and the fruit of thy ground, and the fruit of thy cattle, the increase of thy kine, and the flocks of thy sheep. Blessed shall be thy basket and thy store. Blessed shalt thou be when thou comest in, and blessed shalt thou be when thou goest out. The LORD shall cause thine enemies that rise up against thee to be smitten before thy face: they shall come out against thee one way, and flee before thee seven ways. The LORD shall command the blessing upon thee in thy storehouses, and in all that thou settest thine hand unto; and he shall bless thee in the land which the LORD thy God giveth thee. The LORD shall establish thee an holy people unto himself, as he hath sworn unto thee, if thou shalt keep the commandments of the LORD thy God, and walk in his ways. And all people of the earth shall see that thou art called by the name of the LORD; and they shall be afraid of thee. And the LORD shall make thee plenteous in goods, in the fruit of thy body, and in the fruit of thy cattle, and in the fruit of thy ground, in the land which the LORD sware unto thy fathers to give thee. The LORD shall open unto thee his good treasure, the heaven to give the rain unto thy land in his season, and to bless all the work of thine hand: and thou shalt lend unto many nations, and thou shalt not borrow. And the LORD shall make thee the head, and not the tail; and thou shalt be above only, and thou shalt not be beneath; if that thou hearken unto the commandments of the LORD thy God, which I command thee this day, to observe and to do them: And thou shalt not go aside from any of the words which I command thee this day, to the right hand, or to the left, to go after other gods to serve them.

Chapter 3 — Warning #3

Beating This Evil

WHY PREPARE?

As Christians, we have the most powerful covenant with the Almighty God. We are not the broken-down. We are not the poverty-stricken. We are not the sick and dying. We are the most powerful creatures who walk this planet. There is not a creation or a creature more fierce, more awesome, more fearsome, more conquering, or more dominant than an actual breathing, walking and talking, fire-baptized, Holy Ghost-filled believer.

Hey, there is a devil. There are demons. There is terror. There is wickedness. There are vile diseases and nasty things. But greater is He that's in me than he that is in the world. We're the blood-washed. We're the redeemed. We're filled with the Holy Ghost, and we're powerful. There isn't a sinner alive with more power than us—there is not a tree, a plant, or an animal alive that can compare to us. The fiercest animal in his time was the bear, and David said that he beat it. The second fiercest animal the lion, and he beat it as well. There is not a creature, a reptile, an insect, or a mosquito bite more powerful than us. Listen to me—you are the most powerful creature walking this planet—the born-again, Spirit-filled Christian.

I'll tell you what we need for the day ahead—we need to be who we are and quit acting like the people we used to be, because we used to be defeated. We used to be in bondage. We used to be poor. We used to be sick. We used to be depressed. We didn't know God, and we didn't know His Word. That is not who we are today. You and I are no longer yesterday's man or woman—we're going to be the man or woman of God He created us to be today. Can I have an "amen" on that?

DEMONS

Demons are real. Contrary to some people's belief, demons are not the spirits of humans who have died. We have no verses for this whatsoever. When a man dies, he goes to one of two places. A Christian goes to be with the Lord, and the sinner to Hades (or what we call the temporary hell). The Bible teaches us that to be absent from the body is to be present with the Lord—not roaming the earth.

Demons are alien entities from the region of the damned. Simply said, they are fallen angels. They are sometimes called evil spirits or unclean spirits. Throughout the Bible we see that they are labeled by what they do. For example, there is a demon called an "unclean spirit." This spirit will make you feel unclean, think unclean, talk unclean, look at unclean things, visit unclean places with unclean people, and end up doing unclean things.

Deceiving spirits can be both demons and human spirits. Many people are deceived by them. I have discovered that though many of God's people will rebuke demons, they will also give attention to unrighteous people. If the demons can't get to them supernaturally, they will get to them through unrighteous people who are influenced by the same demons. People can say no to the devil but can't say no to people. The only reason the devil can get away with this scheme is because the body of Christ keeps falling for it. We must watch for this trickery.

Ephesians 6:11

Put on the whole armour of God, that ye may be able to stand against the wiles of the devil.

These evil spirits are real, and they are everywhere. They are mostly ignored; therefore they roam freely among us. We must do something immediately to stop them from having free access into our lives. They must be addressed, and they must be dealt with. I am not one to make a big deal of demons, but at the same time I do know they are present and they can be bound. I must voice my concern here that most Christians do little or nothing about this, and most pastors seldom teach on this subject.

Evil spirits will be a part of everyone's future because they are running rampant on the earth, and we live on the earth. Scripture after scripture warns us about this. Even so, they should have no place in our lives and absolutely no access. We should not act like them or talk like them. They should have no influence on us.

It strikes me as strange that while demons roar against even the Church, the Church is getting more and more quiet about demons and less and less discerning about their activities.

WEAPONS OF OUR WARFARE

Without a doubt, we will need these supernatural weapons to do spiritual warfare and survive the times. We are supernatural people, and we should be living supernatural lives. Our warfare is not natural; it is spiritual (2 Cor. 10:4–5). The enemy soldiers are invisible and must be dealt with. Our weapons are not common to man, but they are mighty through God. Our emphasis is stayed on the Lord, yet we must be aware of any attempt of the devil to gain entrance into our lives and get him back under our feet.

People who are filled with the Holy Spirit have nine supernatural weapons (gifts of the Spirit) listed in 1 Corinthians 12:7–10. If you are not filled with the Spirit, you have basically two supernatural weapons—the name of Jesus and the Holy Scriptures. If you include the blood of Jesus as a weapon, you have that also. However, if you are a Spirit-filled Christian, you have these three powerful weapons of war, plus the nine gifts of the Spirit. We also have the armor of God. These weapons of war help us to be supernatural warriors. They give us a tremendous advantage over the devil and his evil spirits. They allow us to see into the spirit realm and therefore allow us to function in that realm. The devil hates this. With these weapons, we outmaneuver him, and we never fall prey to him. In fact, many times we overpower him.

Remember, our enemy soldiers are invisible and supernatural. They must be dealt with through the power of God and the weapons of our warfare.

ARMOR OF GOD

Ephesians 6:11-12

Put on the whole armour of God, that ye may be able to stand against the wiles of the devil. For we wrestle not against flesh and blood, but against principalities, against powers, against the rulers of the darkness of this world, against spiritual wickedness in high places.

There is absolutely nothing in the entire world that is more beneficial to the believer than the armor of God. There is no argument that God Almighty gave us this armor to protect us as we live on this planet surrounded by all types of enemies. It is also very powerful because it protects all of our biblical spiritual systems.

I have taught on the armor of God for many years. I have also heard it taught in many different ways. I do not so much concentrate on the individual components of armor, as if it were for an ancient knight, but rather on what each piece of armor means to us and provides for us. I will explain this a little further in the next chapter but for now, realize that you must get this armor functioning in your life—and you must do it now.

KEEP YOURSELF

It is more than fair to say that if you do not keep yourself "Christian" and maintain your Christian walk, you will be much more vulnerable to the attacks of the enemy on every front of life.

1 John 5:18

We know that whosoever is born of God sinneth not; but he that is begotten of God keepeth himself, and that wicked one toucheth him not.

This verse alone is enough to warn us to take care of ourselves and maintain our Christian walk. The phrase "keepeth himself" is referring to you and me, the everyday believer, to maintain our Christianity. Living in these last days, I have noticed that many churchgoers are religious on Sunday but do not live it Monday through Saturday. Don't tell me for a second that the devil is not paying attention to this. We also learn from this great verse that the wicked one cannot touch those who maintain a disciplined, biblical, and dedicated life in the Word and prayer.

I think we all know that to be a Christian is more than a belief system or a new doctrinal experience. It is a life-changing, lifetime walk of being transformed into His glorious light, denying the world and refusing to be conformed to this world.

1 Peter 5:8-9

Be sober, be vigilant; because your adversary the devil, as a roaring lion, walketh about, seeking whom he may devour: Whom resist stedfast in the faith, knowing that the same afflictions are accomplished in your brethren that are in the world.

I want to point out here that the devil cannot just march into your life and devour you. You must give him some permission. This verse does not say that the devil walks about seeking whom he wills to devour but rather whom he **may** devour. If we obey the scriptures that tell us to maintain our Christian walk, he has no permission to enter our lives. If we do not live steadfastly according to Christian standards, he receives that as our permission to function in our lives. As simple as this seems, many people never, ever get a grip on it, and that is why the devil continues to ransack their lives. And yes, I'm talking about churchgoers too.

It is our responsibility to maintain our Christian walk. The devil is not omnipresent or omniscient (like God), and he cannot be everywhere at one time. He is forced to mobilize his demons to move about the earth to harass us. We must resist him by being steadfast in Christianity. If we do everything the Bible tells us to do as Christians, we give no place to the devil.

Some believe it is legalism or bondage to be required to live a certain biblical lifestyle or live up to specific biblical standards; however, we have discovered that this is not so. The Lord is telling us to blockade the devil and every one of his tricks and schemes designed to hurt our lives. If there is no sin, deception, seduction, unforgiveness, etc., there is no food for the evil spirits. I believe it was Dr. Kenneth E. Hagin who once said, "Flies do not land on hot stoves." I suppose an entire book should be written on this subject, but for now we must move on.

No matter the cost, keep all sin out of your life, and keep your entire life in line with the Word of God. Obviously this is easier said than done but absolutely possible. Christians who have gone before us have proven it, and many who are among us now live a very biblical, disciplined, and clean life.

POWER OVER DEMONS

Before we go to the verses, I want to give you a brief word of explanation. The Word of God consistently warns us about these invisible enemy soldiers and their deceitful maneuvers. We must have an ear to hear what the Spirit of God is saying to the Church. I am not of the belief that every little thing that goes wrong can be blamed on the devil or demons. Although I totally believe they exist and that they are very active in the earth today, I do not believe they can just march into our lives and have their way or override our will.

I realize that in times past there were those who overemphasized some of these doctrines and perhaps were even a touch fanatical about how they dealt with evil spirits. I have never endorsed anything that is an "overemphasis" and don't intend to now. I do not overemphasize the devil or his demons, neither do I ever include them in my prayers or address them with my eyes closed, my head bowed, or in any other way that could be interpreted as though I'm showing them any respect whatsoever. At the same time, I realize they are lurking in the shadows, potentially stalking any one of us at any time, to hurt us or to destroy what is ours. It is fair to say that we must do something to blockade these demons from entering our lives.

I have included a couple of verses to remind you what the Scriptures say about our power and authority over evil spirits—to cast them out, to bind them (handcuff them and stop them from functioning), and to loose people who are bound by them. I know many people who "verbally abuse" the devil (almost cursing him) and constantly give him extra attention. However many of these same people live ransacked lives, and it is obvious that all of their name-calling is not stopping these evil spirits from harassing them.

The Bible is clear about how to stop them. My brief teaching about living a steadfast, Bible-based life and being spiritual is one of the greatest ways to resist the devil and cause him to flee from you.

Mark 16:17

And these signs shall follow them that believe; In my name shall they cast out devils; they shall speak with new tongues . . .

Luke 9:1

Then he called his twelve disciples together, and gave them power and authority over all devils, and to cure diseases.

Luke 10:19

Behold, I give unto you power to tread on serpents and scorpions, and over all the power of the enemy: and nothing shall by any means hurt you.

Mark Barclay Ministries often receives calls from people requesting help and information about how to deal with evil in their lives. Many of them say they have seen a manifestation or have actually experienced a supernatural being speaking to them. Many of them say that the evil spirit brought fear with it and left a dirty feeling in the room after they left. You can hear in their voice that they are not just saying these things but actually did experience some kind of encounter with an alien entity.

When we ask them about their Christian walk, most of them (not every one of them) reply with a less-than-favorable report. In fact, if we were keeping a good record, they would probably have Ds and Es on their Christian report card! It normally does not take me long to determine why the devil is harassing someone's life and what brought them to their current condition, simply by evaluating the broken hedges in their life, the words of their mouth, and their relationships.

Without a doubt, it is the will of the Lord God that we defeat every enemy of life, supernatural and natural, and live under the blood covenant. It is the will of our Father that we are conquerors and live a life of freedom—not freedom **to** sin but freedom **from** sin.

STRONGER THAN YOUR ENEMIES

Psalm 105:24

And he increased his people greatly; and made them stronger than their enemies.

Throughout my Christian life I have clung to this verse many times. I am absolutely, without a doubt, convinced that this is the will of God for us. Increase means you don't have it all yet, but it is coming. Increase means that we are growing stronger and stronger. Increase means that God has advanced us, fortified us, and added to us. God is going to continue to have this role in our lives until we truly are stronger than all of our enemies. This is not too good to be true—it is exactly where all of us are headed.

Never, ever, never give place to any evil spirit, practice, or people. Do not go to those places where evil is practiced or be around those who practice it. Fight every element that causes you to decrease and tries to pull you away from God.

It's obvious the Lord Jesus wants us to be safe and protected. He wants us to be able to blockade all evil—all sickness, disease, evil spirits, evil people, and any other element that could maim us, destroy our lives, or deny us the opportunities to live in His blessings.

I encourage you (no, actually I challenge you), in the name of Jesus Christ of Nazareth, to not just be a churchgoer, but be one who is actually living this new life every day—a life for which Jesus Christ paid a price; a life free of sin, struggle, pain, sickness, and all evil; a life of victory, peace, joy, and righteousness in the Holy Ghost.

In the following chapters, I will provide more details about some of the things you can do to prepare yourself for the day ahead.

The Holy Spirit

THE SEVEN MOST NEEDED THINGS

In this chapter and those that follow I am going to tell you the seven most important things you can do to prepare yourself for the day ahead. Please understand that I am much more of an optimist than a pessimist, however I also understand that the Scriptures clearly paint the picture of evil and dangerous days ahead.

If you can just master these seven things in your life, you will most likely stand strong, even in the darkest days that lie ahead. You will be much better off than those who do not know to do these things. If these seven things are understood and practiced every day, they will totally blockade the devil. Once you get into these chapters, you will realize that many other elements and issues of life fall under the canopy of these.

The purpose of the power of God is not just to help you be a good church member. It is to help you be powerful in life. It is the will of God that you conquer and master life and not allow life to conquer you or become a slave to circumstances, poverty, and other people. Slavery of any kind has never been of God. It isn't even humane, let alone divine.

HOLY SPIRIT POWER

Acts 1:8

But ye shall receive power, after that the Holy Ghost is come upon you: and ye shall be witnesses unto me both in Jerusalem, and in all Judaea, and in Samaria, and unto the uttermost part of the earth.

Let's look at this a little more closely. **You shall receive power** after that the Holy Ghost is come upon you (and in your case, **in** you—He lives **in** you), and you shall be witnesses for Jesus Christ. It begins at home and then as your influence ripples out (like a rock plunging into a lake), it affects more and more people—all the way out into the uttermost parts of the earth. This means as far as your life reaches and as far as your journey takes you.

I would like to point out here that this verse deals with our being witnesses. This is not so much just refering to being a **verbal** witness but actually **being** a witness. Obviously this is talking about our lifestyle. It is referring to how Jesus Christ has changed our lives and how He has made us different from our neighbors.

The work of the Holy Spirit is to make us godly. He guides us and leads us out of evil and temptation and into the wonderful things of God. He has been assigned to help the Father's dreams for our lives come true.

Let's also look at this word "power" for a moment. This is referring to God's power, not natural power. This is referring to having more power than all the power of the enemy. If you want to do a great study sometime, look up all the words on power and authority. This will not only get your attention, it will also build you up. I've listed just a handful of verses for you to meditate in, and perhaps they will inspire you to study further.

Matthew 10:1

And when he had called unto him his twelve disciples, he gave them power against unclean spirits, to cast them out, and to heal all manner of sickness and all manner of disease.

Mark 3:15

And to have power to heal sicknesses, and to cast out devils . . .

Mark 6:7

And he called unto him the twelve, and began to send them forth by two and two; and gave them power over unclean spirits . . .

Luke 10:19

Behold, I give unto you power to tread on serpents and scorpions, and over all the power of the enemy: and nothing shall by any means hurt you.

John 1:12

But as many as received him, to them gave he power to become the sons of God, even to them that believe on his name . . .

Romans 15:13

Now the God of hope fill you with all joy and peace in believing, that ye may abound in hope, through the power of the Holy Ghost.

2 Timothy 1:8

Be not thou therefore ashamed of the testimony of our Lord, nor of me his prisoner: but be thou partaker of the afflictions of the gospel according to the power of God . . .

2 Peter 1:3

According as his divine power hath given unto us all things that pertain unto life and godliness, through the knowledge of him that hath called us to glory and virtue . . .

JESUS HAD POWER,
NOW WE ALSO HAVE POWER

Praise God, look at Acts 10:38 with me:

How God anointed Jesus of Nazareth with the Holy Ghost and with power . . .

He not only had the fellowship of the Holy Spirit, but He also possessed His power. If you and I could ever get a grip on this! If I could ever come to the place of realizing that I am not subject to what Mark knows. I'm not subject to what Mark has seen. I'm not subject to Mark's education. I'm not subject to Mark's ability. Are you listening to me? I'm a temple of the Holy Ghost. I don't know everything, but I'm in close fellowship with the One who does. I'm in fellowship with someone who knows everything. Who is that? Jesus. And by His Spirit, praise God, I've got the power. You've got the power. That's what it says—you're going to receive power. "I'm believing for that, Brother Barclay." Do you have Jesus? Are you filled with the Holy Spirit? Then you've got the power. "But I don't feel like it." Let me help you. Acts 1 didn't say that you will receive a feeling you've got power. It just says that you've got power.

You and I need to realize that we have power, and we must learn how to release it. That's the key part about this verse. God, the Father, anointed Jesus of Nazareth with the Holy Ghost and power. Now watch what happened when Jesus received the Holy Ghost and power. It says that He went about **doing** good. When you receive the Holy Ghost, it is difficult to sit still. You have to train yourself to sit still. I don't mean that you cannot sit and learn or be patient. I mean you want to do something. You want to be involved in something. You want to "pay God back." Once you receive this power, you want to do something productive for the Lord because it's not just about commanding demons or praying in tongues. No, the purpose for the power is not just for church life. The purpose for the power is to be a witness and to conquer sin. The purpose for the power is to conquer evil. The purpose for the power is to conquer depression, discouragement, fear, and the things that drag you down every day. The power is not so that we can feel powerful in church. No, it's for every day. It's for the lowest moment of the lowest day that you have faced this month. That's what we have, and it causes us to go about **doing** good.

When you receive the Holy Spirit on the inside of you, all of a sudden you don't want to gossip anymore. You don't want to hold grudges anymore. You don't want to fight with people anymore. When you see hurting people you say to yourself, "What can I do to help you? What can I do to heal you? How can I get you out of that?" Someone asked me, "Brother Barclay, how did you grow a ministry like this?" I said, "I don't know. I started out caring about someone else and saying to Vickie, "Honey, let's talk about that family. What are we going to do? What do you and I possess or what can we do to help get that family out of that trouble, to get them out of that pain, to get them over this thing? There must be something you and I can do—give, pray, say, visit, anoint—something that'll get that guy or that family out of that thing. I don't want them in pain anymore."

When you meet Jesus—Compassion Himself—you are consumed with His heart, and your heart is supernaturally changed forever and ever. I don't know where you're coming from, but I am the guy who hated people. I am the guy who didn't like humans. I did everything to hurt people. In high school I fought guys I could beat, and I fought guys I couldn't beat and just figured that even if they beat me, I'll get in a lick or two anyway. I even swung on teachers. It's nothing to be proud of. I used to hate people. And then I met Jesus of Nazareth, and all of a sudden my heart began to turn. It isn't from the outside in. It isn't a training course you go through. It's not a class you go through. It begins in the heart, and all of a sudden you say, "I don't want to hurt that guy. He made me mad, but I'm done hurting people. I don't want to hurt that guy; I want to help him." Then it grows in you. The closer you get to Jesus, the more you see hurting and suffering people and say, "I'm going the extra mile. There's got to be a way." That's what Jesus did.

Prior to receiving "this" anointing, Jesus was seen sitting with the doctors of the law, debating the Word. Nothing wrong with that! He was always the Son of God, but after He was anointed with the Holy Ghost and power, we see Him doing miracles. And every miracle Jesus performed was to rescue someone. It was to establish someone. I'm going to say that differently—every miracle Jesus did was to rescue someone else, to heal someone else, or to set someone else free. Jesus was the most liberating person on the planet. He delivered people from sin, bondage, slavery, sickness, disease, and the devil himself. This Jesus lives inside of you and me. Now you tell me, how on earth can you walk through this spiritual journey on this planet, with Jesus inside of you, baptized in the Holy Ghost, having all of these spiritual weapons and spiritual gifts at your disposal, yet remain bitter and mean, hate people, gossip, become a talebearer, and want to hurt people? There's something wrong! That's right, there's something wrong. And it's not something wrong with the Lord.

We're the power-packed ones. We're anointed, just as Jesus was anointed. We're not Jesus, so we don't need to be anointed for what He did. Let me help you—Jesus was anointed to die for you. He was anointed to take your sins upon Himself because He had no sin. He was anointed to beat temptation, and He fell to none.

HIS CROSS — YOUR CROSS

Jesus was anointed to lay down His riches and His stance in the heavenly places to take on the form of a servant so that you might become rich. That's what the Bible says. The Bible says He became poor. He wasn't raised poor. He's God. He left golden streets and supernatural, heavenly threaded robes and the purest gold upon His crown to become like you and me in this form of a servant. He was tortured and killed for you. That's His cross.

The Bible says it's time for you to pick up your cross. You might say, "What's my cross, Pastor? Am I to die for the cause?" No, you are supposed to live. His cross was dying; your cross is living. His cross was taking sickness and disease upon Himself. Yours is to receive your healing and minister His healing power to others. His cross was to pay the price for your deliverance from bondage, temptation, and sin. Your cross is to live without sin and bondage and to beat temptation. His cross was to lay down riches and become poor and pay the price for your prosperity—not just survival money but more than enough to get ahead in life and finance the work of Christ, exceedingly above and beyond whatever you can ask or think. Jesus was anointed to do His part of His work, and you are anointed to do your part of His work. No, you are not anointed to be the Messiah. No, you're not anointed to be the Savior. No, you're not anointed to be the Healer or the Great Physician. The Bible clearly defines your anointing: Freely you have received; now freely give. What does it say? Go tell everyone, heal the sick, cleanse the leper, raise the dead. That's our anointing!

"But, Brother Barclay, I don't feel anointed." Well, you are. We are the anointed ones. We're called by God, and we must quit living like we're the downtrodden, the beaten, the ditched, and the beached. That's not us. We have a gift from Heaven, and we need to quit fooling around with life and start addressing life (not according to what we feel, not according to what we discern, not according to our knowledge, not according to how we were raised, not according to the temperature or the weather, and not according to our circumstances). We need to address life according to the Word of God.

You military people know this. It's always easier to just go in and take the real estate and pay whatever price is necessary to secure the perimeter of whatever coordinates they're giving you—just secure that thing and take charge of it and run the enemy off. That's tough, I know. There may be some very strong enemies, and it could require a high price to accomplish the assignment. However, that is much easier than to lose it to the enemy, and then a day or a week or two later have to turn around and climb back up the same hill, get to the same mountaintop, and go back and get that same piece of territory or go back after the same island again. The island's the same, and the enemy's the same. You're the one who is different. You've been there before.

We are the blood-washed. We are the fire-baptized. We are the born-again crowd. We're the most fearsome, the most awesome, and the most powerful Bible-believing creatures who ever walked this planet, for greater is He that's in us than he that's in the world!

WALKING IN THIS POWER

Yes, I'm going to walk in this power God gave us. Amen. It's more powerful than whatever you're facing. Just name something. It's more powerful than sickness. It's more powerful than pain. It's more powerful than disease. It's more powerful than high cholesterol. It's more powerful than triglycerides. It's more powerful than high blood pressure. It's more powerful than diabetes. It's more powerful than cancer. It's more powerful than unemployment. It's more powerful than poverty. It's more powerful than lack. It's more powerful than my enemies. If you and I are going to journey through this life (and we are), we might as well journey through it as spiritual giants, causing sinners to respect us and demons to run from us—not the other way around.

In the name of Jesus, get the Book out and let it guide your path like a light, all the way through troubled times. Thank God for His Word! Your Bible is not just for carrying; it is your weapon. It is the sword of the Spirit. There is no demon, depression, discouragement, bitterness, unforgiveness, grudge, prejudice, pride, arrogance . . . there isn't a sickness, disease, disaster, pain, or crisis . . . there is no unemployment, poverty, or lack . . . no greed, lust, or sin that this sword cannot repel. This is not a sword fight to see who's the best. You pull this sword out of your heart and project it through your lips, and the enemy pulls back—immediately. The problem is that because of spiritual laziness, most Christians don't actually do this. They only believe it.

I challenge you, in Jesus' name, to pick up your weapons and stand up and address the issues that are clobbering your life. Stop saying, "I guess I'm just going to have to live with it. It's just the way I am. I guess I'm just always going to be this way. They say there's no cure, and I've done this and tried that, been there, done that. It's just me." We're going to shake off this spiritual laziness and battle fatigue. Amen! We're going to address these issues with the Word of God. We're going to talk about how big God is.

Back to Acts 10:38:

> *How God anointed Jesus of Nazareth with the Holy Ghost and with power: who went about doing good,*

and healing all that were oppressed of the devil; for God was with him.

I like that it says He "went about doing good" and healing all of those who were plagued with sickness or disease or had a demon that was oppressing them. When this anointing came upon Jesus, He went about "doing good." You cannot help but do the same when the anointing gets on you. You could say that this is the effect of the anointing. The less anointing you have, the less energy and determination you'll have. The less anointing you have, the less power you have to overcome the obstacles of the day. The more anointing you have, the more you find yourself doing God's work and being about your Father's business.

Take a look at these verses with me:

Acts 1:1–5

The former treatise have I made, O Theophilus, of all that Jesus began both to do and teach, Until the day in which he was taken up, after that he through the Holy Ghost had given commandments unto the apostles whom he had chosen: To whom also he shewed himself alive after his passion by many infallible proofs, being seen of them forty days, and speaking of the things pertaining to the kingdom of God: And, being assembled together with them, commanded them that they should not depart from Jerusalem, but wait for the promise of the Father, which, saith he, ye have heard of me. For John truly baptized with water; but ye shall be baptized with the Holy Ghost not many days hence.

MANY INFALLIBLE PROOFS

When God moves on your behalf, you have infallible proofs. It's not just a story. It's not just a feeling. It's not just discernment. You have proofs that are infallible and though they may be challenged, they will always be proven true. I have proof that I'm a Christian. Hundreds of people who live less than an hour from here knew the old Mark Barclay, and now they have met, seen, tasted of, and can't believe that I could be the same guy—can't believe that a demon-possessed boy really could become a godly man and do the work of God. I have infallible proof that I'm a blood-washed, born-again Christian. Hallelujah—many infallible proofs!

There are times in certain meetings that I stand my son up beside me, who was never to be born. When Vickie became pregnant with him, it was totally contrary to the doctors' reports. We were told more than once that not only would Vickie never be able to deliver children again but that she should do everything in her power to never become pregnant again. When she became pregnant for Josh, the reports changed. We were then told that he would be born either incomplete or deformed. These words, "He'll never live" and "Vickie will die delivering him" constantly ran through my mind.

When the two of them stand at my side, Josh doesn't look deprived to me at almost 6 feet 2 inches tall! He's smart, he graduated from high school at fifteen, he was ordained before he was eighteen, he works with me at my right hand, and he loves God on his own. I don't have to whip him into it. Vickie didn't just "survive" this challenge; she conquered it. She is fine. She was fine on the delivery day, and she is even better today. Jesus is Lord over the Barclays!

You and I have many infallible proofs that our God is alive, and He's in our lives today. It's not a story I'm telling. I have proof about what God has done in my life today, and so do you. "To whom also he shewed himself alive . . ." (Acts 1:3). The Lord is alive. He's alive and well, with many infallible proofs.

Acts 1:8

But ye shall receive power, after that the Holy Ghost is come upon you: and ye shall be witnesses . . .

You shall receive power that's going to turn you into something. You're going to receive power from the Holy Ghost, from the presence of the Holy Ghost, and that power's going to turn you into something. What's it going to turn you into? Witnesses. This is not power to be a verbal witness only. Do you know what a witness is? A witness is someone who saw something. A witness is someone who heard something. A witness is someone who has evidence. This verse just said that once you receive the baptism of the Holy Ghost (that's you and me—the Spirit-filled Christian), you'll have this power to **be** a witness (not just say that you are). Everywhere you go, you will be a living epistle and a witness—someone who has seen the Lord, someone who has talked to the Lord, someone with whom the Lord has had fellowship, and someone who has experienced a miracle the Lord has done on your behalf. You will become this witness, once you receive the power of the Holy Spirit. Give Him praise for it!

I'll tell you what we need for the day ahead—we need more Holy Ghost presence in our personal lives to keep making us into this powerful witness He wants us to be—living, awesome, fearless conquerors of this planet, mastering life and coming out of every trial and every tribulation saying, "I have proof that I walk with God, and here it is" (and tell your story).

We are not the broken-down crowd. We've got to quit looking like it. Our countenance should not look like we're losing and don't know what to do next. You may feel like you're losing. It may look like you're losing. You might not know what to do next, but that doesn't change you. Things change; you don't. If all hell (meaning every demon power) broke out against you and just started ransacking your life and chasing you and messing with you, it might change your money, it might change the house you live in, it might change how high the grass grows . . . a lot of things can change, but it should not change you. It does not remove the blood-washed benefit from your life. It does not erase your water-baptism. It does not take away the Holy Ghost from guiding you and leading you. It does not erase this power that lives on the inside of you. We're the conquerors. It's time to conquer. We're the victorious. It's time to have some victories. We're the commanders.

Think about this now. We should not be fearful—we're the fearsome. Demons should look at us and say, "Oh, no, do you mean to tell me one of those Christians is moving into this neighborhood? Before you know it, they're going to be praying in the yard and singing out of their windows and witnessing to the neighborhood and carrying Bibles in and out of their car, and . . . oh, no, not in this neighborhood." It shouldn't be the other way around, "Oh, my God, I'm a Christian and there's a demon chasing me." We must reverse this role. Amen. Say, "Greater is He that's in me than he that's out there in the world."

Come on, this is not just good preaching. This is not just a good thing to say. This is not who we're becoming. I'm telling you, this is who we are—the blood-washed, the water-baptized, and those who are filled with the Holy Ghost. We have power that no sinner possesses to cast out demons; to tread upon the spirits that are trying to ruin our lives; and to rebuke poverty, debt, and unemployment right in the face.

We can do one of two things, friends. All of us have the same opportunities. Go home; open up the envelopes; take out the phone bill, the light bill, and the other bills; and meditate, worry, frown, pout, get fearful, lose your faith, and wonder where your God is—wonder what you're going to do next, and walk around the house saying, "I don't know what I'm going to do. I don't know what **I'm** going to do. I don't know what **we're** going to do. Oh, my God, what are **we** going to do?" Or we can release this wonderful power in our lives, the power of the Holy Ghost, while He makes us into these domineering, conquering creatures who walk across the earth to reap the souls of men, which is the highest commodity.

THE ARMOR OF GOD

You need the leadership of God, meaning that you need to hear from Him and do what He says and not argue with Him all the time. I'm telling you, if you don't have what I'm teaching in these next few paragraphs, your tomorrows are going to be very troublesome. For the day ahead, you and I need the armor of God (the armor of God, not your armor), and we need to know how to put it on.

God created you with natural armor to protect yourself in the natural world. Your natural armor is your immune system; the skin that covers your flesh; and the ability to reason, calculate, summarize, determine, and decide. These are all part of your armament. Do you understand that? You already have God-given armor that protects you from the elements. You can absorb a certain amount of radiation, and your body can repel it. It won't hurt you. If you absorb too much, you go beyond your protection. You can deal with a certain level of bacteria and repel it, but if you take on too much, you will have longer-lasting symptoms.

You also have supernatural armor to protect you spiritually. Why do we need this kind of protection? Because the day ahead will bring a lot of spiritual enemy activity, and there's a lot of spiritual warfare even now. So let's study about this armor of God, what it is and how to put it on.

Ephesians 6:10-12

Finally, my brethren, be strong in the Lord, and in the power of his might. Put on the whole armour of God, [not just part of it] *that ye may be able to stand against the wiles* [tricky ways] *of the devil. For we wrestle not against flesh and blood . . .*

What is flesh and blood? People. Our warfare is not with people. If we're having trouble with people, we don't want to concentrate on that and start getting into strife and division and quarreling and bickering and blaming someone else while they are blaming us. That is not our warfare. Say out loud, "That is not my warfare." My warfare is against principalities, powers, the rulers of the darkness of this world, and against spiritual wickedness in high places. Our warfare as Christians is spiritual. It is in the spirit realm, and it is against spiritual enemies. That's the kind of warfare we're supposed to be fighting.

Ephesians 6:13-14

Wherefore take unto you the whole armour of God, that ye may be able to withstand in the evil day, having done all, to stand. Stand therefore . . .

What does that mean? I've done all to stand. Why does the Lord want me to stand some more? This verse says that after YOU have done all that YOU can do to stand (or to withstand this thing that's attacking you) . . . now stand in the armor of God. He's not just telling you, "Don't quit." The Lord's saying once you've done everything that you can do, step out of your own ability, put on the armor of God, and make a stand in God against this thing. "Lord, I've done all I know to do, and now I'm going to make a stand in God."

For example, the helmet of salvation is a supernatural benefit that allows us the God-given ability to have the mind of Christ. I believe it also helps us to deny our own thoughts, fears, insecurities, and the other elements that would stop us from being the bold, supernatural warriors God expects us to be.

Another example is the breastplate of righteousness. I simply interpret this as the God-given powerful ability to keep our heart clean before God. No hurt feelings, no unforgiveness, no bitterness, and so on. These issues of the heart can cripple many good, Christian people and eliminate any opportunity for victory.

As you study each of these pieces of armor, you can see that God has truly covered us and equipped us for battle. He has thoroughly prepared us for any area through which these invisible enemy soldiers might try to get to us. The armor of

God also protects us from the unfair and hurtful elements that humans could use to attack us. You can study the armor of God in Ephesians 6. I will give you a quick list here, but I highly recommend that you look into this more thoroughly.

1. **The Belt of Truth**
   a. The only real truth is the Word of God.
   b. We live by truth.
   c. We speak the truth.
   d. We're to be known for truth.
   e. We are filled with the Spirit of truth.
2. **The Breastplate of Righteousness**
   a. A clean heart—no guile.
   b. A heart after God.
   c. No unforgiveness.
   d. No bitterness.
   e. A realization that you are right with God because of Jesus Christ.
3. **The Boots of the Preparation of the Gospel**
   a. Trained in the Word of God.
   b. Constantly studying the Word of God.
   c. Speaking what the Word says.
   d. A pastor making you into a disciple of Jesus Christ.
   e. Feet that no longer take you to mischief.
   f. The ability to stand on His Word, no matter what.
4. **The Shield of Faith**
   a. Walking by faith and not by sight.
   b. Believing the Word over your circumstances.
   c. Believing in your heart what God has said.
   d. Speaking with your mouth what you believe in your heart.
   e. Walking accordingly.

5. **The Helmet of Salvation**
   a. Renewing your mind with the Word of God.
   b. Being transformed by the renewing of your mind.
   c. Being conformed to His image.
   d. Putting on the mind of Christ.
   e. Not thinking like a natural man but a supernatural man.
   f. The supernatural ability to cast down every thought that does not line up with the thoughts (Word) of God.
6. **The Sword of the Spirit**
   a. The written Word of God.
   b. The Rhema Word of God.
   c. The spoken Word of God.
   d. Putting the Word in your mouth and speaking it forth with authority.
   e. Speaking forth the name of Jesus, according to the Bible.

Obviously there is much more that could be taught here about each one of these points, and they could be defined with greater detail, but this will give you a brief list so you can determine if these things are working in your life.

THE VOICE OF GOD

It is very difficult to be led by the Spirit if you do not hear His voice. I have said for many years that one of the greatest things for a believer to do is learn how to hear the Master's voice. The voice of God in our lives is not just for prophecy in the congregation or even to comfort us when we're going through tough times. It is also meant to bring us warning and instructions and even commands from Heaven.

After Jesus ascended to the Father, He continued to need a commander over the apostles and issued commands to those whom He had called. This is still one of the ministries of the Lord Jesus Christ. If you look this up in your Bible, you will notice that in Acts 1:2, Jesus does this through the Holy Spirit.

One of the greatest protections we have is the ability to hear His voice so we can receive His commands and obey them to the degree that God could literally warn us to step off an airplane, not knowing it's going to crash, or to tell us not to enter a building, not knowing it's about to be bombed by a terrorist.

This voice of God in our lives can also guide our steps into our future and help us raise our children, knowing in advance what the Lord has for their lives. Developing precision in discerning God's voice will certainly lead us safely during these perilous times, away from perilous people, and keep us out of danger.

We see throughout the entire Book of Acts how Jesus (through the Holy Spirit) interacts with the disciples and apostles of the day, guiding them and leading them in every area of life. We also see that it wasn't always just endorsement. We understand that many times the Holy Spirit ordered preachers to go to certain cities and forbade them to enter others. If you want to be prepared for the bad things that are coming down upon the earth, you must walk with God on this level.

Perhaps it goes without saying that many people are too busy, their lives are too cluttered, and they are caught up in too many other things, but I am going to say it anyway—people are too busy, their lives are too cluttered, and they are caught up in too many other things! It is starting to break them down, deteriorate their protection systems, and make their lives unstable.

THE HOLY SPIRIT'S MINISTRY IN OUR LIVES

The Holy Spirit has several ministries in our lives. He is alive and well on Planet Earth, and He lives on the inside of us. We are the temples of the Holy Ghost. Here is a quick list with references, designating things we can expect the Holy Spirit to do in us and through us. Take some time to study each one of these before you read on until you get them deep into your spirit.

1. John 14:26
   He will teach you all things.

2. John 14:26
   He will bring to your remembrance all things that you have been taught.

3. John 15:26
   He will be known as the Spirit of truth in your life.

4. John 15:26
   He will testify of Jesus and constantly confirm your salvation in your heart.

5. John 16:13
   He will guide you into all truth.

6. John 16:13
   He will speak to you only those things from Heaven.

7. John 16:13
   He will show you things to come.

8. Acts 1:2
   Jesus will come into you through Him.

9. Acts 1:8
   You will have a special God-given power that other humans do not have.

10. Romans 8:14
    He will father you and treat you like a son of God.

11. 1 Corinthians 6:19
    He will supernaturally live on the inside of you.

12. 1 Corinthians 14:2
    He will give you a prayer language so you can communicate directly with Heaven, without any man or any evil spirit knowing what you are speaking to God.

There are other things we could list here, but I suppose this is enough to inspire you to dig deeper and convince you that we are not mere humans. We are absolutely spiritual in God and the most fierce, supernatural beings to ever walk on this planet. We are living in the last days, and we are not alone. We know this by faith, we know this by the Scriptures, and we also know this by the witness in our very inner being.

No offense intended, but I feel there are those who are in need of this great impartation of the Holy Spirit. Many of our more modern churches have, as I call it, kicked out the Holy Spirit. In a teasing way, I sometimes say that they have taken the Holy Spirit to a back room somewhere and duct-taped Him. In other words, many people believe they are Spirit-filled and attending a Spirit-filled church, but there is absolutely no remaining sign or evidence that this is actually true. Surely they do not realize that the Holy Spirit and God are one. If you are ashamed of the Holy Spirit, you are ashamed of our God. If you're ashamed of His presence or the manifestations of the Spirit, you are ashamed of our God. If you shut out the Holy Spirit or don't welcome Him, you have shut out our God and He is not welcome. If you feel that the great Holy Spirit and His manifestations are embarrassing to the visitor, you are ashamed and embarrassed of our great God.

As we close out this chapter, I'd like to remind you that having this powerful Holy Spirit in our lives is one of the greatest things you can do to prepare for anything that would come down upon this earth, including all the filth and evil that lies ahead. **"More Holy Spirit than ever before!"**

Chapter 5 — Protection #2

he Preacher

A HOLY GHOST, GOD-FEARING PREACHER
WHO FEARS GOD MORE THAN YOU

A dear friend of mine and one of God's greatest generals, Dr. Lester Sumrall (now in Heaven), was famous for the saying, "You can have what you preach—and you will." With this in mind, we look forward to the future, knowing that it is the strong preaching of the gospel that will set people free and enable us to conquer the times. There may be no one more important in your life than your preacher. There may be no one connected to your family and your private life more important than your pastor.

As I mention throughout this book, the last days are upon us. We can no longer say they are coming one day in the future. They are here now, and we are living right in the middle of them. Why is it that many of our preachers are abandoning sound doctrine? Some are preaching that there is no hell, others that we are already living in the millennial reign, and even others are refusing to declare that Jesus Christ is the only way to Heaven.

Romans 10:17

So then faith cometh by hearing, and hearing by the word of God.

1 John 5:4

For whatsoever is born of God overcometh the world: and this is the victory that overcometh the world, even our faith.

Every Christian everywhere knows that faith comes from hearing the Word of God preached. Yet in these last of the last days, from the same Christians, we are seeing less and less severity about church attendance. The Bible tells us in Romans that they will not hear without a preacher, and the preacher is in the house. Simply said, when you come to church and hear the preacher preaching the Word, a supernatural event happens. This supernatural event is the release of faith into our hearts. This faith is what overcomes the things of this world and causes us to conquer them and have the victory.

You would think that as Christians learn this they would drastically improve their church attendance. I have noticed most recently that the local church is being frequented less and less. Many times the Word content is so watered down and so brief that little faith is released. A simple equation—little hearing equals a little faith, which equals a little victory. The reason this is not good enough is because most people have big problems and need big faith to have victory over these big problems.

Turn in your Bible to Acts 7:51, and get ready to read. One of the things you're going to need for the day ahead is a bold, God-fearing, right-living, Holy Ghost preacher. You're going to need a preacher who walks with God.

A PASTOR IS A GOOD THING

I remember a heart surgeon friend of mine once told me that during the years he grew up, his daddy told him that everyone needs three things to be a success. One is a good medical doctor who knows what he's doing because, sooner or later, throughout this life, having babies, raising kids, and dealing with stuff, we're going to need a good doctor. His dad also told him that everyone needs a good lawyer. If we're going to be successful, make money, and become a professional, sooner or later we had better know a good attorney for our business affairs. The third thing his dad told him was that we've got to have a preacher who knows God, and God must know our preacher.

His daddy sat him down and said, "Son, there are things a preacher can do for you that no other person on this planet can do for you. As you have kids and grandkids and raise your family and one day bury your mom and dad, you will need a friend who talks to God."

The important point here is that my heart surgeon friend was not a Christian man, and neither was his dad. Here's a sinner man telling his son, "Let me give you some advice, son—you must have a preacher in your life." If a sinner knows that, surely a Christian should realize that you must not walk into the darkness of the future without a preacher who knows God, and God must know the preacher. Notice how I said it—a bold, God-fearing, right-living, Holy Ghost preacher, who fears God more than you. And I meant every word of it. That's what we need for the day ahead.

JESUS, THE PREACHER

Now let's read Acts 7:51–53:

> *Ye stiffnecked and uncircumcised in heart and ears, ye do always resist the Holy Ghost: as your fathers did, so do ye. Which of the prophets have not your fathers persecuted? and they have slain them* [these preachers] *which shewed before of the coming of the Just One; of whom ye have been now the betrayers and murderers: Who have received the law by the disposition of angels, and have not kept it.*

I like the way this preacher preaches. He doesn't mess around. Wow! Where do you go today to hear that kind of sermon? Most preachers are afraid they might offend someone, scare someone away, or that someone might say he's hard, too straight, or too bold. I have even been accused of being legalistic or that I'm preaching bondage. Today, boldness is misinterpreted as arrogance and cockiness. Actually it's confidence. I am not preaching bondage. Bondage is being bound to or by something. Good, confrontational preaching exposes satan's schemes and sets people free. I am trying to get people free from the things that have them bound. Weak preaching keeps people bound and even teaches them to remain in their bondage. Weak preaching implies that Jesus doesn't care if people stay bound and that they have special permission to keep on sinning (and stay bound) because they are under grace.

SIN STRIPS YOU OF YOUR CONFIDENCE

Sin strips you of your confidence. If you're not living in sin, you've got a bunch of confidence. Are you listening to me?

This preacher, Jesus, stood right up to them, and He basically said, "You listen to Me—you're stiff-necked, and you're uncircumcised in your heart." Some believe that's a tough sermon, but I was studying one day about my favorite preacher of all times. Of all the preachers I've studied and read about, my favorite preacher of all times is a young man from Nazareth, and His name is Jesus. (By the way, when they told Him it was okay to start preaching, no one was ever the same again!) He was a strong confronter—from the woman at the well (talking to her about her private life) to the public rebuke to the Pharisees. He was honest, bold, and confrontational.

Weak, anemic, selfish, carnal, arrogant, churchgoers today (not that all are) say that their private life of sin is none of the preacher's business. But I'll tell you that if a preacher follows the example of Jesus, he makes it his business. Jesus asked that woman at the well some pretty personal questions. Jesus preached straighter, rebuked and confronted more, and went after people's sin more than all the other preachers in your Bible. It wasn't because He was mean, hard, had no love, and had no shepherd's heart (or any of the other phony, exaggerated sayings that sinning Christians use to protect their sin and still try to keep God in their lives).

Many people truly believe that their roots and their culture trump the Word of God. This is by far not true. There are no verses to substantiate this belief. Though it may be important to some people, it is not scriptural. We are to leave our way of living and be converted to His way. We are to be conformed to His very image. The Book of Romans says that we are to no longer be conformed to this world but be transformed by the renewing of our minds.

If we allow everyone to bring their culture into Christianity and set a precedent that their cultural practices are permitted, it will be devastating. First of all, many of our roots and cultural traditions are not biblical whatsoever. They have just been handed down from our forefathers. On the other hand, there may not be anything "wrong" with a certain tradition, but it must be subjected to the Word of God.

Many modern preachers are presenting a walk with Christ that is totally pleasing to the congregation, regardless of whether or not it lines up with the New Testament. This is not only hurting people's lives, but as they cast off restraint, the enemy is striking something fierce. The true biblical preacher patterns his ministry after Jesus Christ. His preaching is patterned after the messages that Jesus preached. The true biblical preacher is helping people get free from sin, its pain, and its penalties. Many times I have said that I am free **from** sin, not free **to** sin. I told a preacher the other day that I have been water-baptized for the **remission of** sin rather than the **permission to** sin. Besides that, I can't imagine why anyone wants the world or enjoys sin. I have been totally delivered from it and have found great strength and freedom in having no vices and no attachment to the world, the flesh, or the devil.

2 Corinthians 6:17–7:1

Wherefore come out from among them, and be ye separate, saith the Lord, and touch not the unclean thing; and I will receive you, And will be a Father unto you, and ye shall be my sons and daughters, saith the Lord Almighty. Having therefore these promises, dearly beloved, let us cleanse ourselves from all filthiness of the flesh and spirit, perfecting holiness in the fear of God.

The reason Jesus' preaching was so straightforward and even confrontational is because He loved people and He knew the danger, harm, and pain of sin. He knows the cost of sin when it's not dealt with, when people just let it grow in their garden and in their life. It was out of love and compassion that this preacher from Galilee, Jesus, preached the way that He did. Amen. He wasn't hard-hearted. Many times He would minister to individuals, taking a blind man aside or traveling all the way across the lake to cast demons out of just one person. Jesus was, at times, soft and compassionate and gentle as a dove but at other times bold as a lion.

Let's remember, Jesus was the preacher who had the Pharisees and the high priests and Sadducees right in His congregation, pointed them out to His disciples, and said (paraphrased), "Beware of the leaven of this group right here, the ones who sat right here, the Pharisees. Boys, you beware of them. Don't listen to them. And over here, snakes and serpents." That is the King James language from the mouth of Jesus. He didn't say, "Hey, there are snakes. We ought to talk about this in private." Oh, no! He said, "You row of snakes and serpents, and you—you white-washed sepulchers. You're all pretty on the outside, but you're nothing but dead men's bones on the inside." That's the kind of preaching Jesus did. No wonder the religious people wanted Him crucified. But the sinners said, "We find no fault in this man." The "church" crowd of the day said, "Get rid of this guy. Who does He think He is, talking like this?" Those were the "church" people of the day, the religious people. But the sinners were attracted to Jesus. They knew He was for real. No one preached like Him. They knew there was no private gain in preaching like this.

What you **do not** need for the day ahead is a preacher who will stroke you, pet you, put a Band-Aid on your wound, or help you sin. Shame on any preacher who will help you ditch one woman and love another, help you ditch one man for another, and so on. (I'm talking here about people who just pick and choose. We don't judge you if you were sinned against or your marriage fell apart. But there are some people who go from one person, to another person, to another person, etc.)

You need a preacher who will tell you straight. First of all, almost no one is in church long enough or often enough. Those are two different things—long enough and often enough. Most people are not in church long enough and often enough to really allow a pastor to make a disciple out of them. As pastors, we are hoping that you're studying your Bible at home and purging and dealing with yourself. "Lord, I don't want to smoke anymore. I don't want to drink anymore. I want these cuss words out of my mouth. Lord, please help me. Like Pastor taught last Sunday, I'm going to pray every morning. I'm going to get rid of this." As pastors, we are taking for granted that you are doing this. If you believe the local church is some kind of emergency room where you can come in once on Sunday morning, pay a little money, say a little prayer, receive a blessing, and then go out and think everything's okay, your pain is going to continue and be long-term. The longevity of your life is going to be cut short. Evil is going to come upon you in these last days, and you're not going to have what it takes to repel it or bounce back from it. This is not what I want for you, neither am I cursing you. I am warning you that the worst evil that modern man has ever known is about to come upon this earth, even upon many churchgoers and those who call themselves Christians. You must possess the power of God to repel it and deal with it, or you'll be stuck just coping with it and possibly even be destroyed by it.

This is Paul talking to the Church of Corinth:

1 Corinthians 2:3-4

And I was with you in weakness [humility], *and in fear* [the fear of the Lord], *and in much trembling* [I wanted to do good and obey God]. *And my speech and my preaching* . . .

Speech and preaching—these are two different things. My everyday speech (my everyday conversation) is one part of my life, and my pulpit speaking is another part. You should be able to run into your preacher anywhere around town, and he should not seem like an entirely different person. He might not be dressed in a suit, and he might not have a sermon on his lips. Ministering the Word from the pulpit is one thing, but we must also have a "Bible worthy" mouth at all times. No, I don't mean that we should walk around and do nothing but quote verses to each other. Some people are like this—I am not! I don't just go around quoting scriptures all the time. One time I asked a person, "How are you doing, brother?" "Like a tree," he answered. "Pardon me?" I asked. He said, "Like a tree, planted by the rivers of water. My leaves shall not wither, and whatsoever I do shall prosper." I greeted another person and asked, "Who's with you?" He answered, "Goodness and mercy—they follow me all the days of my life. Here, meet goodness and mercy." Wow! I'm not that way. I'm just a real person, and I believe that real preachers are real people. We have a relationship with God, we walk with God, and we sacrifice our lives to help you become a better Christian. We pray with you and stand with you and help you and walk with you. While you're walking out your salvation, we're walking out our salvation as well.

Say this with me, "I am a real person. I face some real problems, but I serve a real God who has real solutions, and He's really moving on my behalf." I live by that, and I really do believe that.

MY FIRST PASTOR

I'll always remember my first pastor. I was barely born again and still working for the United States Marines as an instructor at the recruit battalion in San Diego, California, doing most of my work at Camp Pendleton. I attended a small Pentecostal church with a Spirit-filled pastor outside of Camp Pendleton.

I recall watching my pastor handling the believers with "kids' gloves," as if they were frail or fragile. Perhaps they were, but I was not! I went to my pastor and actually said to him, "Pastor, I notice you are treating people here as if they are breakable or will be put out with you. I want you to know that I'm not that way. I need help, and I need it now. I am way behind the others in Bible knowledge and knowing how to be a disciple of Jesus Christ. I want you to make me into a disciple of Jesus Christ, no matter the cost. And please, Pastor, tell me the truth, man-to-man, and don't hold back. I give you my word, in Jesus' name, I will not be offended; neither will I ever quit. Please don't tell a story and expect me to figure out the meaning. Just treat me like an adult. Tell me what's right and wrong, what I should be doing that I'm not, and what I'm doing that I shouldn't. I will submit and obey."

My pastor took me up on this, and it turned into a wonderful relationship. I owe this man so much. The fact that I humbled myself and remained teachable and allowed him to speak directly to me cut out a lot of wasted time. The Lord Jesus used my pastor to deliver me from anger, rage, violence, drunkenness, smoking, foul language, and other things. Thank God for a good pastor!

I never could understand why the body of Christ is so childish and so frail. I guess it's like what Paul referred to—that he had spiritual things to tell the Church but could not because they were still natural people. I pray for you, that you are strong in spirit, that you receive your pastor as the gift of God to help you, and that you can trust him to lead you into green pastures and still waters. I pray for you, that you will humble yourself and be teachable and allow your pastor to reprove, rebuke, correct, and instruct you in right living.

I often think about this powerful verse in the Book of Timothy:

2 Timothy 4:2–4 AMP

Herald and preach the Word! Keep your sense of urgency [stand by, be at hand and ready], whether the opportunity seems to be favorable or unfavorable. [Whether it is convenient or inconvenient, whether it is welcome or unwelcome, you as preacher of the Word are to show people in what way their lives are wrong.] And convince them, rebuking and correcting, warning and urging and encouraging them, being unflagging and inexhaustible in patience and teaching. For the time is coming when [people] will not tolerate (endure) sound and wholesome instruction, but, having ears itching [for something pleasing and gratifying], they will gather to themselves one teacher after another to a considerable number, chosen to satisfy their own liking and to foster the errors they hold, And will turn aside from hearing the truth and wander off into myths and man-made fictions.

I especially like the way the Amplified Bible says, "You as preacher of the Word are to show people in what way their lives are wrong." The reason for this is not to embarrass or humiliate you in any way, neither is it to control you. It is to help you fix the things that are not proper in your life. Every athlete knows the value of having a strong coach who won't mess around but tells you the truth so you can be the best that you can be.

The preacher is not the standard. He's an example. Jesus is the standard, and the Word of God is the standard. You ask, "What's the difference?" The standard never gets sick. An example might, but just watch him walk it out. A standard never has a financial problem, but an example will say, "I'm not only going to be an example when I have some money. Watch me serve God when things are tight." A standard never has a bad day, but a good example says, "Well, I have bad days and I have better days, but watch me serve God whether I'm having a good day or a tough day." That's a good example. The Bible says that preachers lead by example. Make this confession, "Jesus and His Word are the only standards, nothing and no one else." That's right. That's exactly right.

Please understand that I am not teaching (neither do I endorse to any degree) that preachers should be holy and clean in the pulpits and live less than that anywhere else. In fact, I teach and stand for just the opposite. It is a shame to Jesus and rather disgusting to have teachers in the pulpit and on TV who look so pure, yet when out of the pulpit they live worldly and dirty. Shame on every one of them! Shame on those who know about their filthy activities and their worldly lifestyle yet follow them anyway.

Back to the Apostle Paul who said (paraphrased), "My speech and my preaching were not to entice you with wisdom from men but with a demonstration of the Spirit and the power of God."

". . . in demonstration of the Spirit and of power" (1 Cor. 2:4). We must get away from the demonstration of the entertainment spirit and the celebrity spirit that I see on so many ministers today. Sooner or later, the "party church" will come to a close because the party will be over. And many of the "entertaining" speakers will fall to the wayside. They just do not possess the power to help people receive what it takes to beat the elements of the day.

Let's look at what the Bible says about Peter, another great preacher:

Acts 10:44
While Peter yet spake these words, the Holy Ghost fell on all them which heard the word.

This is the kind of preacher we need. When he stands up to preach or teach, he causes you to be able to "feel" it when God begins to enter the house. People get healed under this kind of ministry. People get delivered. There's power attached to the words. You don't need a preacher who is just "wordy." The truth is, it would help many preachers to come down from their education level and speak some common English language occasionally.

Jesus is still building the kingdom of God today. He told stories about mustard seeds, farmers, sowers, plants, and animals. He just kept it really down-to-earth and simple, even though He was so wise that He bewildered the minds of the doctors of the law. Get it straight, Jesus did not give people what they wanted, neither did He teach what they wanted. He taught about simple life issues, filled with the truth and power of God. It seems that many modern teachers have mistaken this powerful style of delivery for being a "man pleaser" and a "human attractor."

You want your preacher to be what the Bible describes a good preacher should be. He should be a Bible person. He should be doing everything (even more than you're doing) to try to live what this Bible says. You should never catch your preacher cheating with substance abuse, smoking, drinking, drugs, or sensual things. You should never catch your preacher with another woman. You shouldn't be able to catch your preacher because there should never be another woman or any other secret sins. A preacher should have already graduated beyond being a beginner disciple, and the elements of the flesh should already be purged out of his life.

Are preachers perfect? No, we're not. We still have to fight attitudes, feelings, hurt feelings, and persecution. But a preacher should no longer be fighting the lust of the world or the things of the world. No, we should be more mature and developed than that. We should be more spiritual than that. We should be submitted to the Word so you don't have to be ashamed of us in the community.

Your preacher should walk with God. He should have results beyond people saying that he's educated. He should be more than funny. He can use humor, but he'd better have something deeper than humor. He should be more than a motivational speaker or a purveyor of information. Your preacher should be a man (or woman) of God. He should be known for his walk with God. He should be committed to prayer. When you need someone to pray, you should have confidence that if you can just get your request to your pastor, he'll pray. You should have a preacher who is there for you.

You should know in your heart that your preacher lives a separated life. Though he knows people in the community and political officials and people in high authority, he doesn't live like them. We know where our preacher is—he's with his wife, he's in his pulpit, he's in his Bible, he's in prayer. If he has a hobby or a craft or something he enjoys doing, it shouldn't be something shady or something that has any sign of worldliness that makes you wonder if he's carnal. (The most carnal thing I do is squeal the tires on my hot rod once in a while!)

There are different descriptions in our minds of what a pastor's role and duties are, which are normally formed by how we were raised, our culture, what kind of church we were brought up in, or what we have been taught. Just because each denomination requires a different role for the minister, it doesn't mean they're correct. We must learn what the Bible says about it and go with that, and only that.

I tell our church family all the time that I am their pastor and I love them. But really, they know and I know that Jesus is the Good Shepherd, and I'm just an undershepherd who works for Him. God appointed me to take care of them. I'm on His payroll. He hired me to feed them the Word of God and to teach, preach, pray, prophesy, and be here for them. I don't run when the wolves come, like a hireling. You want a preacher who is going to be faithful and who is going to stick with the cause and stick with the mission. If you read through the Bible, you can find some good examples.

I don't want a preacher like King Saul, who was afraid of the people. I don't want a leader who is afraid of the people and gets everyone in trouble with God. There may be a couple of whiners or a couple of church bullies who want to do things a certain way. If the preacher is afraid to confront them or say no, then everyone will end up going the way of the bullies and whiners, instead of the way of God.

I don't want a preacher like King David. David was an adulterer. David was into live porn. He peeked over the balcony on purpose. Actually, he didn't just peek—he gawked and stared. David was a murderer. David gave the order to have one of his own soldiers placed in harm's way so he could sleep with the guy's wife. You don't want a leader like David. David stuck up for his son Absalom when he broke not just one rule but every rule—right in front of everyone else. On the day of his son's death, David put on this big scene, "Absalom, my Absalom." No, you don't want a preacher like David. I guess David did have at least one good quality. The King James Version tells us that David had a heart after God—not a heart "like" God's but a heart that "chased after" God, even when he sinned. For that we give him great credit.

You don't want a leader like Ananias. He was a fired-up leader in the church, but he and Sapphira fell in love with the money and ended up cheating God over it. They lied to the preacher and the Holy Spirit.

You don't want a preacher like Korah. He'll lead you right into the pit. He led two hundred fifty in one day to the judgment of God. They all went to hell alive.

You don't want a leader like Simon, the sorcerer, who thought that because he had money and favor and prestige, he could somehow purchase the anointing of God.

I don't want a preacher like the rich, young ruler, who was very interested in and wanted to be a ruler in the kingdom of God but wasn't willing to pay the price. I want a preacher in my life who is continually willing to pay the price for the gospel ministry.

You don't want a Demas. Demas was a leader on the Apostle Paul's team, but Paul said, "Demas has forsaken me, because he fell in love with this present world."

You don't want a preacher who makes you wonder if he's in love with God or in love with the world. Does he love what's going on out there, or does he love what's going on in church? I don't want to question that about my preacher. I need to know who and what he loves. I need to know where he's sowing his time. I will know what he's involved in and what he's doing by the way he talks. Amen.

I want a preacher like Paul—courageous, confronting. He'll line you out yet ride aboard a shipwreck to preach the next sermon to the next group of people.

I want a preacher like Philip, who goes and stands in the desert and feels like a nut when everyone is doing great. When they ask what he's doing, he answers, "I'm obeying God, standing in the desert." I want a preacher who obeys God.

I want a preacher like Stephen—bold as a lion and afraid of no one, even when they threatend to kill him. He didn't pause for a moment. He kept going on to the next sentence. (I think their stoning was worthless. Stephen never felt a stone, I can tell you that right now.)

I want a preacher like Simon Peter. He's bold, he's loud, and he's aggressive. When he's wrong, he comes back around and says, "I was wrong, and I love You, Jesus."

I like Peter because, even though he denied Christ, he stayed with the Church. When Jesus rose from the dead and Mary and Martha were the first to see Him, He told them to go tell the disciples that He has risen. Then He adds this little phrase (Barclay version), "And tell Peter, who's up there sitting in the corner, feeling like he's not a part of the church anymore because he publicly denied Me—you tell him he's in." On the day of Pentecost, Peter received the Holy Ghost! That's the kind of preacher I want. He didn't just go start a traveling ministry; he preached to the people before whom he denied Jesus and called them out by name. He said (Barclay version), "I've got a new word for you. Forget what I said before. I'm not denying Him anymore. Let me tell you about my Jesus." And he went about preaching the things of God. Amen!

I want a preacher like Barnabas. He didn't just care for himself; he constantly brought in others. "Hey, you don't know Paul, but he's okay. You guys need to receive him."

I want a preacher like John the Baptist. (Actually, I want to **be** this kind of preacher as well.) John preached some of the coolest sermons! I want a preacher who preaches to sinners just like they are already church people. John got down in that water and looked up and preached to them, "You need to repent and get down here." The entire city came to hear him preach, and most of them were baptized that day. That's powerful. That's what you need for the day ahead.

I don't know where your path is going to take you. It's your path. I know where my path is going to take me because I've made straight paths for my feet. Most of the issues of my life are already decided upon. I don't know if you've become that decisive about your life—what you're going to be and where you will do it. I just know my own life that well. Wherever life leads you, I hope you're smart enough to stay in a church where there's a real preacher and not a Hollywood, tinseltown preacher; a Disney Land jokester; a *Reader's Digest* quoter; or a poet. I hope that whatever you do in the days ahead, you always stay with a bold preacher who will tell the truth, remain in God's house, stay in the Word of God, and just keep studying.

The day of the hireling is over. We will always have those who are greedy and use the gospel for gain, but coming soon will be the realization that this game is over. I'm sure we'll always have the foolish Christians who keep falling for gimmicks and tricks. I realize there will always be unrighteous people and unrighteousness preachers, but they won't be the majority. I realize we live in a day like Sodom and Gomorrah and the day of Noah. Jesus said this would be the condition of the day and the condition of society when He returns. Even so, I see people hungry for God Himself, for His power, and to live in His mighty presence. This is a day of cleaning house for the "pulpiteers!"

If you are called or plan to preach the gospel, I highly recommend that you read my book, *Preachers of Righteousness*. I call you blessed today, in the name of Jesus.

Lord, I pray that You will sow this message right into our hearts and help us. I claim this for every one of us. I want to be this kind of preacher, Lord, and I want to have this kind of preacher over my life. I want all the preachers who work with me and around me (and those who will grow up under my oversight), to be Bible preachers with no ulterior motives. We're not weak people; we're strong! We're lovers and forgivers, and we're going to bring strength to other people's lives. I thank You for it, in Jesus' name, amen.

Chapter 6 — Protection #3

he Church

I know that some people will look at this chapter and perhaps not even read it because they have convinced themselves they don't need a home church. As a matter of fact, many are even deceived about the subject. They don't understand that the local church is the ark of safety. We live in the day that will usher in the great judgment, just like in the days of Noah.

Luke 17:26-27

And as it was in the days of Noe, so shall it be also in the days of the Son of man. They did eat, they drank, they married wives, they were given in marriage, until the day that Noe entered into the ark, and the flood came, and destroyed them all.

Luke 17:28-30

Likewise also as it was in the days of Lot; they did eat, they drank, they bought, they sold, they planted, they builded; But the same day that Lot went out of Sodom it rained fire and brimstone from heaven, and destroyed them all. Even thus shall it be in the day when the Son of man is revealed.

In the day of Noah, everyone but eight people had turned away from God. The judgment came, and only eight survived.

Noah rescued all eight of his family members (including himself), and I believe the reason is because they helped build the ark. I will remind you that only Noah had a word from Heaven (not his wife, and not one of his children), yet they all remained faithful to building the ark of safety. Those who built the ark of safety rode the ark of safety and survived the judgment.

In the day of Lot, things were similar, as we just read in verses 28 and 29. Lot was able to rescue only himself and two of his family members, his two virgin daughters.

When God was going to judge the cities of Sodom and Gomorrah, Abraham interceded for the righteous. The angels were sent to warn the righteous, which, according to the Word of God, were only Lot and his immediate family. When the angels placed an urgency in the heart of Lot to leave the city immediately, his heart was drawn away to his other two daughters who were married to young men in the city. (I've heard some preachers say that they were not even married, just living together.) Lot went to these other two daughters who had married sinner boys from the perverted city. His sons-in-law scorned and mocked him. They were just too calloused and filled with the world to pay any attention to any warning from God or from Lot. He lost them and his two daughters in the judgment.

Lot, his wife, and his two virgin daughters began their journey to leave the city, barely escaping the judgment. At the edge of town, Lot's wife disobeyed God by looking back and was caught in the fiery judgment. The cost of chasing the dream that says "the grass is greener on the other side" finally sank in, and the Scriptures say that Lot's righteous soul was vexed daily. Lot had moved to the green pastures and valleys outside of the sinful cities of Sodom and Gomorrah, believing that prosperity was the answer to all things. Come to find out, the prosperity was there, but it snuggled up to the filth of this world. It was not the prosperity itself that got Lot and his family—it was the filth connected to it.

Isn't that something! Noah rescued all eight family members, while Lot was only able to rescue three (including himself). Why are we writing about Noah and Lot? Because the Scriptures are clear that the day of the Lord's coming will be just like the day of Lot and the day of Noah, as we have already shown you in the previous verses.

I know with everything in me that those who help build the ark of safety (the local church) will escape the judgment and help usher in the climax of the last days. However, I have a deep warning from God that everyone else will be in a heap of trouble, terror, and torture. I beg of you, please receive my warning and don't make light of it.

Believe it or not, you must faithfully attend a good church to survive the day ahead. Many people will not like this chapter because they have already made up their mind that they don't need church. I've even heard people say recently that churches are the pastor's idea. I am sad about this because all of the unchurched people I know are among the weakest people I know. There is an old philosophy that if the seas are dangerously rough and rocking the ship to the point of damage, do not jump out of the boat, thinking that you, by yourself, are stronger than the vessel.

With all of my heart I encourage you to find a good church, where the Word of God is preached without compromise and the Holy Spirit is present, and stay in that local church, no matter what. This is almost a guarantee that you will successfully ride out the storms of life.

A GOOD CHURCH

I've been writing about things you need for the day ahead. Say it with me, "Things I need for the day ahead." You and I have entered that day, and there are certain things we must take with us.

Let me repeat myself, please. In the day ahead, you're going to have to know that you are in a good church. There are certain elements in church that are found nowhere else. I've determined that most people don't even know what a good church is, let alone whether or not they are attending one. Many people will discard a good church simply because there's someone there who hasn't treated them well or they didn't have a good time. We need to make sure that we don't disqualify church life or abandon our church because of a personality conflict, a disagreement, or someone we don't like. Maybe you didn't get your own way, and the other person did. Maybe there is a dispute that isn't settled yet. That doesn't mean that your church is not a good church.

JESUS WENT TO CHURCH

Jesus went to church as a lifestyle. It was His habit. Let's look at a couple of verses:

Luke 4:16–17

And he came to Nazareth, where he had been brought up: and, as his custom was [underline that in your Bible, if you haven't already], *he went into the*

synagogue on the sabbath day, and stood up for to read.
And there was delivered unto him the book of the
prophet Esaias. And when he had opened the book, he
found the place where it was written . . .

It was about Himself of course. I use this verse to say to myself, "Listen, Mark, if Jesus went to church as a custom, tradition, habit, and **lifestyle**, you should go to church." If Jesus (the Son of the Living God, the Christ, the Messiah) found it necessary to attend church and either read the Book or listen to the Book being read and be baptized by John for the sake of the fulfillment of the Scriptures, how much more do you and I need to understand the need to attend church as a habit and a lifestyle?

I LOVE CHURCH

I am a product of the local church. I was not raised in church, but since I met Jesus Christ, I love to be in His house. I like everything about it. Attending church is one of the greatest joys of my life. It has been a tremendous place to raise my children and now watch my grandchildren grow up in the things of God.

I am completely convinced that the only way to truly succeed today and in the day ahead is to be grounded in a local church with a good pastor. I know there are many believers who disagree with me about this, but I "know that I know that I know" that this is true. I am observing that people who attend church less and less are becoming weaker and weaker and more and more carnal.

Not too long ago, I was interviewed by the famous sports-caster, Pat Summerall. It was a personal interview about my life and success as a leader in my field. It was aired on CNN on a special program called Summerall's Success Stories. At the conclusion of the interview, Mr. Summerall asked me to share one of the greatest secrets of my life, something I believe has contributed to my success. Without any hesitation, I answered, "Pat, once I met Jesus Christ, I immediately went to church and after all these years, I have never allowed anyone to chase me off!"

Don't misunderstand. I know church life is not always easy for many people. There will always be people there who are not completely fixed yet, and certainly not everyone is spiritual all the time. Some people have bad experiences with some of these immature or carnal Christians.

Other people have issues with the leadership—a lay leader, department head, or sometimes even their own pastor. No matter what people do or try to do to you, there is nowhere like the house of God. Never, ever, never let anyone push you away from God's house and His holy altars.

Hebrews 10:23

Let us hold fast the profession of our faith without wavering; (for he is faithful that promised . . .

Who promised? Jesus, the Lord, and the One who promised is faithful to His promise.

Hebrews 10:24

And let us consider one another to provoke unto love and good works . . .

We shouldn't provoke one another to fight, pick on each other, and get into strife. We should provoke, but we should provoke one another to walk in love and to do good works. Isn't that wonderful?

Hebrews 10:25

Not forsaking [don't forsake!] *the assembling of ourselves together, as the manner of some is . . .*

This verse tells us two things. Number one, don't you do it! Do what? What other people are doing. What are other people doing? That's number two—they are forsaking the assembling of themselves together.

Some ask if they can just meet in a home with a couple of friends. The Bible does say that anytime any two or three of us are gathered together in His name, there He is in the midst of us. So yes, two people can stand in the desert and agree in prayer, and the Lord will honor that and answer that prayer.

But **gathering** together and **assembling** together are two different things. Gathering is simply, "We're getting together—want to come over? We're including you to join the four or five of us who are getting together," or "Come on, kids, we are gathering together now as a family." That's gathering.

Assembling is more formal. It is planned and purposed. When you assemble something, it means you're putting it all together. When the church assembles together, it means that everyone is coming together—every head of household, every second head of household, etc. We have Papa Bear, Mama Bear, and Baby Bear. That's the Bear family, and we also have all the other families. We all come together, at the same time, for the same purpose. We are assembled. When we're all together at the same time for the same purpose, we don't just gather together and have a gathering—we have an official, formal assembly together. The Lord looks down from Heaven and says, "I see them in their homes, I hear them in their cars, and I see them on their jobs." But what a sight for the Heavenly Father when He looks down and sees the church family assembled together, all worshiping Him and singing unto Him and bringing in the tithes. The Heavenly Father receives great pleasure from seeing what we do while we're assembled together in His house—whether we're singing, praying, communing at the Lord's table, teaching, praying for each other, or anointing with oil.

I don't know how well you know your Bible, but one verse says that He inhabits the praises of His people. This means that when we're assembled together and praising Him, He gets so involved, He decides to come down in the midst of us and love on us and "hug" us, His children. It's important to the Lord that we come together so He can look down and see His entire family together. It's a weekly family reunion for the Heavenly Father. It's a wonderful thing.

I sometimes think that maybe the Lord Jesus is a little embarrassed. As He's seated at the right hand of the Father and looks down into the sanctuary, He turns to His left, and there's the Heavenly Father, and He says, "Well, Father, there are fifty other families that belong to this church family, but I couldn't get them in Your house today to worship You. They call Me 'Lord,' and they call You 'Father,' but I couldn't get them here. I'm very sorry about that." Now, I don't know for sure if that's how it works or not, but that's what I would think if I were sitting at the right hand of the Father and I were responsible to present the church family to God, without spot or wrinkle or blemish.

My report would be embarrassing: "Well, Lord, they want to go to Heaven. They just don't want to go to church. They're too busy. They love You but not enough to sacrifice their own goals and motives."

It seems that sometimes we only think about what helps **us** and relieves **us** of whatever pressure **we're** in, but I believe we need to consider that the Lord is looking down upon our lives and whether or not He is pleased.

Jesus went to church consistently, as a lifestyle. That's a pretty good reason to go to church. We're not going to forsake church services. We are going to the house of the Lord, and we're going to be counted among those who don't just **say** they love God but **demonstrate** their love.

JESUS IS THERE

Let me tell you one of the coolest things about church— Jesus is there. Let me tell you another cool thing about church—you're there. Let me tell you what I love about church—it makes me feel clean and fresh. It provides freedom from the world. A good church service erases the nasty things you pick up in the world. When you go to the job, they flirt with you, they pinch you, they wink, and they talk dirty. It depends on where you work, of course, but there may be things around you that are sensual. When you come to church, it's like this big eraser wipes the slate clean. A good church is like a decontamination station. It cleanses us from all the pollutants of this filthy, antichrist world.

WE ARE ALL THE SAME THERE

Proverbs 22:2

The rich and poor meet together: the Lord is the maker of them all.

Where else do you do that? The answer is nowhere. The rich meet together among themselves, and the poor meet together among themselves, but the two groups do not meet together. In God's house, the rich and the poor meet together, and the Lord is the maker of them all. Do you know what that means? When you come to church, the Lord doesn't care if you're rich or poor because the church isn't a bank.

When we're at church, we're all the same. We're all brothers and sisters in the same boat, wanting to get to the other side. Out there in the world there is wickedness, evil, hatred, prejudice, push-and-pull struggles, differences, and competition. Married couples have issues with single people. Single people have issues with married couples. It's amazing how deep these things can go, and most don't even see it. But when you come into God's house, it doesn't matter whether you're fat or skinny, tall or short, blue-eyed or brown-eyed, dark-skinned or light-skinned. It doesn't matter whether you're from the sixth grade or the sixteenth. All of our accolades and all of our achievements and all of our accomplishments (or the lack of them) mean nothing when we step into His house. We are all the same—blood-bought, blood-washed believers. We're there for one purpose—to be a family in God and become a better disciple of Jesus Christ.

No other place and no other building on the planet has this purpose—not the auditorium (it has its own purpose), not the ball stadium (it has its own purpose), and not the grocery store. No building you ever walk into has the same presence or the same atmosphere or even the same noises as church. Where else can you go where everyone who comes can sing together (perhaps with two or three people you don't know or even like!)?

Where else can you go where everyone is received and treated with respect, regardless of who or what you are? God's house is a magnificent house. The Heavenly Father made it a refuge. The Bible calls God's house a refuge and a fortress. It's a sanctuary. What does that mean? It's a protected arena where no one is supposed to get hurt. No one there is supposed to be picked on. Everyone has equal rights. Some may have more authority than others because of their assignment to help the rest of us. (You can't be responsible unless you're given authority, so some of us do have more authority.) But no one is any better than anyone else— period. The only big guy at church is Jesus Christ of Nazareth.

PRAY AND BE PRAYED FOR

You're going to need church in the day ahead so you can come to pray and ask for prayer. You can pray anywhere you want to, and you can pray for anyone, anytime and anywhere you want to, but you'll discover very rapidly that most people do not pray in too many places, especially where you can just join hands and pray—except for church.

You need a church for the day ahead because it's the only place on the planet that's used for nothing but worshiping

God and getting close to Him. When you bring your kids to church, you're teaching them to worship God and get close to Him. However, you have a free will, and you can form your own opinions. You can bring your kids to church and raise them up, right in God's house, yet allow them to cheat by not attending children's church or not joining the youth group because they think it's not perfect. Understand that this will only hurt them in the end. One of the reasons you'll need the church in the day ahead is to have a place where there is no worldliness, no lust, and no willful sin. You can bring your children and teach them how to worship God, and all of you as a family can get close to Him.

IT IS WHERE YOU PRESENT YOUR TITHES

You must have a church to present your tithes. The Bible says to **bring** your tithes and offerings, not **send** them. You must **bring** your tithe. You're going to need a church in the day ahead because you're going to need the benefits of tithing (your biblical tithers' rights). You're going to need the church to set this system in motion on your behalf. You can send your offerings to other ministries, but you should go to church with your tithe in your hand and worship God with it as a family.

The tithe was set up for multiple purposes and benefits. One of the greatest is the protection system God gave us. If you tithe properly, God rebukes the devourer on your behalf. Powerful! The devourer isn't always the devil—it is whatever is devouring your life at the time. If you would enjoy more biblical teaching about this, you may want to read my book, *The Real Truth About Tithing*, or my audio series, *Tithers' Rights*.

SPIRITUAL LEADERSHIP IS THERE

You need spiritual leadership. You may have other leadership, but in the day ahead, you're going to need spiritual leadership. You may wonder what's so important about that. Even King Jehoash did that which was right in the eyes of the Lord all the days he had a pastor to instruct him (2 Kings 12:2). I'm not talking about your friend or your prayer partner; I am referring to your pastor and the church elders.

Here's another reason you need spiritual leadership. You and I are going to need the church in the days ahead because of the spiritual adjustments and refocusing that come when you are in God's house. My brother-in-law, Rick St. Dennis (Vickie's brother), said something to me that was so cool. He said, "Pastor, you know why church is so powerful for me? Because I come there, and I get adjusted. I get refocused. I get off a little bit sometimes. I don't mean to, but my thinking gets off a little bit. My motives get off. But when I come to church, something happens. Whether it's your preaching or God talks to me or another brother or sister testifies, something happens that adjusts my focus."

STUDY WITH YOUR PASTOR

You need to study the Word with your pastor. That's why you need a good church. You can read the Bible at home, of course, and you can invite friends over and have a Bible study, but it's not the same anointing level as opening your Bible and studying it with your pastor, whom God has appointed to teach you and help you be a better Christian.

Chapter 7 — Protection #4

The Word

PEOPLE LIVE BY WHAT THEY ARE HEARING, NOT BY WHAT THEY'VE HEARD

They should be doing just the opposite! They should be standing on the Word that they have already been taught which has proven to be effective.

2 Thessalonians 2:15

Therefore, brethren, stand fast, and hold the traditions which ye have been taught, whether by word, or our epistle.

2 Timothy 1:13

Hold fast the form of sound words, <u>which thou hast heard</u> of me, in faith and love which is in Christ Jesus.

If you live by what you are hearing, you greatly increase your risk of deception. You will be prone to get caught up in all the new doctrines and practices of the day. Many get caught up in the news and their daily predictions. I have always asked the Lord to do nothing in this generation without including me. At the same time, I am not going to be misled or turn from the great doctrines I have been taught. I refuse to sacrifice them for modernism or fad doctrines.

I realize that we need to keep "hearing" the Word preached on a regular basis, but we must be discerning to recognize false doctrines and weird new things. We must be able "pick out the sticks and eat the hay."

2 Corinthians 6:17–7:1

Wherefore come out from among them, and be ye separate, saith the Lord, and touch not the unclean thing; and I will receive you, And will be a Father unto you, and ye shall be my sons and daughters, saith the Lord Almighty. Having therefore these promises, dearly beloved, let us cleanse ourselves from all filthiness of the flesh and spirit, perfecting holiness in the fear of God.

These are among my favorite verses, perhaps because I am a delivered man and no longer bound by the things of this world. I have so much for which to be grateful. I know the power of coming out from among worldly, carnal people. It is one of the most beneficial things you can do. Come out from among them, and be separate. This is the command of the Lord, and it brings great blessing to your life.

We are to be busy perfecting holiness in our lives. This is our part. Jesus made us the righteousness of God, but we respond to that provision by fighting to be holy. Holiness is one of the most powerful elements of the Christian life. As you become holy, you show that you are changing from being worldly. The things of the world are falling off, and you are beginning to practice the things of the Lord. This is a wonderful life and very pleasing to the Lord.

It is impossible to be holy without the Word of God. The Word of God is the most valuable and precious thing we have, with the exception of the Lord Himself. Remember, the Bible is not just a book of truths; it is the Word of our God.

OVERCOME THE WORLD

1 John 5:4

For whatsoever is born of God overcometh the world: and this is the victory that overcometh the world, even our faith.

There it is. This is one of the most elementary principles of the faith. Everyone should know this and be operating by it. This is what gives me victory over this world—my faith. This is what causes me to be an overcomer—my faith. This is what beats the terrorist, the murderer, the rapist, and the thief—my faith. This is what beats sickness, disease, and depression—my faith.

There is only one place to get faith. Faith comes by hearing. Faith comes by hearing the Word of God preached. Many people believe that faith comes from reading. Not so. Inspiration may come from reading but not so much faith. Your eyes have never been given the permission to extract faith from what they see, but your ears have been given divine permission to extract faith from what they hear. With this faith (this trust in Jesus and His Word) you can overcome anything in this world.

Romans 10:17 tells us that faith comes from hearing. Romans 10:14 also tells us that we cannot hear or receive this faith without a preacher. If we know that faith overcomes the world and that faith only comes from hearing the Word preached, I wonder why so many skip so much church. With church attendance down, faith will be down. When faith levels dive, we overcome less and less. Before you know it, we have defeats in our lives instead of victories. The less faith we have, the less victories we have.

Get all the preaching of the Word you can, as often as you can. Your faith will be full, and you will be a constant overcomer. If you have defeat in your life, you should first look at the level of preaching you are hearing and make whatever commitment necessary to correct the shortage.

A warning to all is that the devil also knows that faith comes this way. Therefore we must be careful to listen to the right preachers. Deception also comes by hearing, and sometimes by hearing the wrong preacher.

WASHING OF THE WATER OF THE WORD

Ephesians 5:26

That he might sanctify and cleanse it with the washing of water by the word . . .

I use this short verse simply to show you that the Word has a cleansing value. We must be washed by it constantly. The greater the washing, the cleaner we are. It takes the Word of God to cleanse us in this way.

The more Word you have, the cleaner you will be. The cleaner you are, the clearer you think. The cleaner you are, the more powerful you are. The cleaner you are, the less place you give to the devil.

THE WORD WILL GUIDE YOU

Proverbs 4:20-27

My son, attend to my words; incline thine ear unto my sayings.

Let them not depart from thine eyes; keep them in the midst of thine heart.

For they are life unto those that find them, and health to all their flesh.

Keep thy heart with all diligence; for out of it are the issues of life.

Put away from thee a froward mouth, and perverse lips put far from thee.

Let thine eyes look right on, and let thine eyelids look straight before thee.

Ponder the path of thy feet, and let all thy ways be established.

Turn not to the right hand nor to the left: remove thy foot from evil.

9 THINGS TO ALWAYS REMEMBER ABOUT THE WORD OF GOD

1. Listen to it. (preaching)
2. Read it. (study)
3. Hide it in your heart. (meditation)
4. It provides "life" to you.
5. It is health to your body.
6. You must guard your heart to keep it in there.
7. You must guard your mouth to keep speaking in line with it.
8. You must guard your eyes to read it more than other things.
9. You must guard your feet so they walk according to it and no longer to mischief.

THE JUDGE

I have a close friend who is a judge and also a fellow Vietnam Marine combat veteran. One day at lunch I said to him, "I wish my church family could all meet you one day." He answered, "If they will listen to you at church and do what you say, they will never meet me in my court. What you preachers call sin, we judges call crime. The best way to keep them out of my courtroom is to keep them in church and out of sin." So true.

5 TRUTHS ABOUT THE WORD OF GOD

Proverbs 6:20–23

My son, keep thy father's commandment, and forsake not the law of thy mother: Bind them continually upon thine heart, and tie them about thy neck. When thou goest, it shall lead thee; when thou sleepest, it shall keep thee; and when thou awakest, it shall talk with thee. For the commandment is a lamp; and the law is light; and reproofs of instruction are the way of life . . .

1. *Bind them continually upon thine heart . . .*
    Meditate in them, and believe them. Fall in love with His sayings, and cherish the reading of them.

2. *. . . and tie them about thy neck.*
    Tie them to your will. Purpose in your heart that you will submit to the Word of God. Even Jesus told the Father, ". . . nevertheless let your will be done."

3. *. . . When thou goest, it shall lead thee . . .*
    This surely covers the daily commute and traveling mercies.

4. *... when thou sleepest, it shall keep thee ...*
   You will enjoy good rest, plenty of slumber, and safety throughout the night.

5. *... and when thou awakest, it shall talk with thee.*
   Guidance comes early in the day, perhaps even before you roll out of bed.

This is a beautiful life—the Word guiding us and keeping us protected from evil and in peace. It sure feels good to feel good. It sure brings confidence when your heart is filled with God's truths. Confidence and stability are always better than inner turmoil, indecision, and fear. When you trust in the Lord and His Word, you can face anything with greater peace.

16 PRODUCTS OF GOD'S WORD

1. 2 Timothy 3:16
   The Word is profitable
2. 1 Peter 1:23
   Born again
3. James 1:21
   Save souls / Renew your mind
4. 1 Peter 2:2
   Spiritual growth
5. 2 Peter 1:4
   Partakers of His divine nature
6. Acts 20:32
   Builds you up
7. John 8:31–32
   Sets you free
8. Ephesians 5:26
   Sanctifies you

9. Romans 10:17
   Faith comes to you
10. Jeremiah 23:29
    Hammers adversaries to pieces
11. John 15:7
    Guarantees answered prayer
12. Psalm 107:20
    Healing for your body
13. Matthew 8:16
    Cast out demons
14. Mark 16:20
    Signs and wonders
15. Acts 19:20
    Prevails
16. Proverbs 6:20–22
    Leads you / Keeps you / Talks to you

We must study the Word, memorize the Word, read the Word, and attend church as often as possible to hear it preached.

In the front of the *Mark T. Barclay Special Edition Bible* I wrote, "I owe my life to the many believers before me who spent their lives preserving these Holy Scriptures so that I can enjoy them and live by them today. I will cherish them in my heart and keep them before my eyes all the days of my life. I pray they mean the same to you (Proverbs 4:20–23)."

Healing Jesus

I will never forget that day! It was about four in the afternoon, and the phone rang. It was my Vickie telling me that the doctor's office just called with the report on the lab work that she had done a few days back. "I HAVE CANCER," she said. Vickie and I have heard bad reports before, but this one caught us totally off-guard. Those words sunk in deep and fast.

As we sat in the doctor's office the next day and he explained things to us, Vickie said the most powerful thing. She said, "Doc, we are believers. My husband and I preach the gospel. We believe the Lord will take care of me. You do what you do best, and Jesus will do the rest."

I have known Vickie since we were barely thirteen. We grew up together, boyfriend and girlfriend. In fact, she is my very best friend in the whole world. We married May 15, 1970, and have enjoyed what some call a storybook marriage. I have known Vickie to be a very strong woman, but she really caught my attention on this day. She sat there with the doctor and never flinched when he told her the prognosis. She never cried; she never looked down. At first I thought she didn't hear him correctly. But as she spoke, that thought was quickly dispelled. Her voice was strong and sure. Her countenance was sweet, and she put a smile on her face. Again, she told our doctor that Jesus was going to deliver her out of this. This was not denial. She was not being "over religious." She simply believed it. "Doc, we are Christians and we believe God, but we are not the kind of people who walk away in denial or say 'thanks, but no thanks' to medical treatment. Again, you do your part, and my God will do His."

On the way home that day I was very angry—not at God or the doctors but the disease (and yes, the devil himself). How dare he do this right under my nose. As I would glance at Vickie, I thought about all the beautiful times we've had together. I thought about what a beautiful woman she is, inside and out. I just couldn't believe this was happening to my girl.

Then I dealt with the feeling of weakness. This happened on my watch! This is the bride of my youth and my covenant partner. I even said to Jesus, "We don't smoke, we don't drink, we don't live worldly in any way, there is no willful sin in our lives, and we don't have any unforgiveness. How could this happen?"

As we prayed and talked things through, Vickie said another very powerful thing. "I am not going to let this break me down. I am not going into hibernation. I am not going to live whatever days I have left in depression, weeping, and in despair. We will tackle this as we have tackled every other attack against us, and we will do what we tell others to do in the time of trouble—we will cry out to God. It will do me no good to mope and mourn about this. God will intervene, and He will give us a miracle," she said.

For over thirty years we have preached the promises of God directly from the written Word of God. The promise of God is to heal us. Both the Old and New Testaments promise us divine health and divine healing. Of course, divine health is better. It is always better to live a healthy life, never needing any healing. However, no one knows better than us that healing is an awesome blessing from God.

As I write this chapter, I feel the power of God coming upon me stronger and stronger. I want to pray for you right now. If you are sick in any way, pull on the Almighty God as you read the next few words. I pray for you, in Jesus' name, that the Lord will heal you and strengthen you, according to 1 Peter 2:24, which says, "Who his own self bare our sins in his own body on the tree, that we, being dead to sins, should live unto righteousness: by whose stripes ye were healed." I believe with you, right now, that you are healed by the blood of Jesus. I call your body healed, inside and out. In Jesus' name, I curse that disease, and it must die so you can live. Receive His help for you, and enjoy the benefits of bodily atonement through His wonderful covenant, in Jesus' name.

Back to my Vickie . . . .

Night and day, we drew closer to God in prayer and put our lives in His hands. We had decided that as we did what we could and should, He would do His part. You can't do His part anyway, and He won't do yours. Vickie received a list of healing verses from our spiritual mom, Dodie Osteen. She reads these every day, many times aloud. Praise God, the Word works!

There is another day I will never forget. It is the day in that doctor's office when he pointed his finger at Vickie and said, "No cancer; you are cancer-free." Once again, Jesus proved

Himself Lord over cancer. I remember what Vickie said, "Doc, thanks for being such a good doctor. We are blessed to have you in our city, and thank You, Jesus, for giving me my miracle!"

Here are the verses Vickie and I stood on (and in fact, we still do):

Psalm 27:2

When the wicked, even mine enemies and my foes, came upon me to eat up my flesh, they stumbled and fell.

Nahum 1:9

. . . affliction shall not rise up the second time.

This is by far one of our favorite verses. Perhaps it will bring you strength in your day of battle.

Micah 7:8 NIV

Do not gloat over me, my enemy! Though I have fallen, I will rise. Though I sit in darkness, the Lord will be my light.

JESUS IS THE ANOINTED ONE

Acts 10:38

How God anointed Jesus of Nazareth with the Holy Ghost and with power: who went about doing good, and healing all that were oppressed of the devil; for God was with him.

It is the Lord Jesus who has the anointing and the power to heal and deliver us from evil. Thank God for His gifts to us and His wonderful, life-rescuing work at Calvary. In this day, above all other times, we are going to need this healing power.

MUTATIONS AND DISEASES

We would be fools to look ahead without considering the impact that disease, bacteria, and infection will have on humanity. Already we face many diseases for which man has no cure. Every new generation seems to have its own curse. In my lifetime we have seen no real cures for killer-level diseases.

Our antibiotics won't touch the viruses of the day, let alone the ones of tomorrow. As these microscopic enemies (whether bacterial or viral) spread, mutate, and spawn new colonies and invade our bodies, they must be stopped by our immune system, which must be tweaked and also graced by God.

BACTERIA

It is very possible that bacteria will be the vicious enemy we face in the future. Even now we are witnessing many who become deathly sick from salmonella, E. coli, and other known bacteria. What always alerts me is how fast these things spread throughout the country. Not to put fear in you, but what if a disease or a bacterium is deadly? What if it spreads rapidly, and what if we have no real vaccine or medicine to counteract it? Just this one scenario makes us realize we must be close to Jesus, walking in His anointing and in His Word.

I predict that greed will end up ruling the world. We see this spirit already ruining our financial systems globally. It is obvious and disgusting what has happened to many people because their own company or boss ripped them off—not so much by poor decisions but by greed. When enough is never enough, and more than enough is never enough, things break down, people break down, and systems (including banks) go broke.

Why am I writing about this, here in this chapter on healing? Because of two reasons—one is the pharmaceuticals, and the other is the chemically-enhanced growth processes for our food. These two elements alone should drive you to prayer.

As long as we permit pesticides, chemical fertilizers, and growth hormones in our food chain, we will have major health issues across the board. Add all this to the bacteria issues, whether accidental or as a result of neglect, and we have a terrible outcome. Our immune system can only repel so much. As long as the people who grow our meat want to grow it faster (for more profit, of course), we will pay the price in our bodies. I suspect that satan himself is somehow behind the invention and spread of all things that hurt and kill humans, including sickness and disease and their causes. We must learn how to find cleaner food, clean the food that is not clean, and pray over all of it.

1 Timothy 4:4–5

For every creature of God is good, and nothing to be refused, if it be received with thanksgiving: For it is sanctified by the word of God and prayer.

THINGS YOU CAN DO

There are things you can do. You can use wisdom with chemicals in your home and on your body. You can exercise and watch your weight. You can eat nutritious foods, especially organic foods. You can learn which foods are like poison and which foods bring life. You can get proper sleep and rest. You can drink plenty of clean water. You should study all of these things because every one of them could extend your life.

You can also pray. You can find healing verses and speak them every day. You can believe God and if you do get sick, you can call the elders of the church. They will know what to do, according to James 5.

You can forgive everyone for everything. Unforgiveness and the spirit of revenge are among the number one reasons people become sick. Also, stay out of strife with everyone. The Apostle Paul warned us about how this could cut our lives short (1 Cor. 11:29–30). Be sure you are walking with God and that you handle His things with respect and hold them sacred.

There is so much to say to you here, but I must keep this chapter short so I will have space to include the others. I have included some special verses here, which will help you be strong and believe for your healing. May you make it through the last days, and may you do it protected, in great health, and victorious.

Study the remaining verses carefully, and commit to memory as many as you can:

1. Luke 4:40–41
   Jesus healed and delivered.
2. Matthew 12:15
   Jesus healed them all.
3. Luke 6:19
   Jesus healed them all.

SEEK HIM FOR HEALTH AND HEALING

3 Stories From the Book of Mark

1. Mark 2:1–5
   His friends tore off the roof.
2. Mark 5:24–34
   She had an issue of blood for twelve years.
3. Mark 10:46–52
   Blind Bartimaeus called out even the more.

8 Healing Avenues From the Bible

1. **The Word of God**
   Psalm 107:20
   He sent His Word.
   Proverbs 4:20–22
   The written Word is health to your flesh.
2. **Laying on of Hands**
   Mark 6:5
   Mark 16:18
3. **Gifts of Healing**
   1 Corinthians 12:9
4. **Anointing Oil**
   James 5:14
5. **Blest Cloths**
   Acts 19:12

6. **Prayer of Faith and Prayer of Agreement**
   Matthew 18:19
7. **Praise and Worship**
   Luke 17:15
8. **Recovery**
   Mark 16:18

The Promise of God for Healing

Isaiah 53:5
Healed by His stripes

The Fulfillment of Healing by Jesus

Matthew 8:14–17
He did it.

The Witness of the Apostle Peter That It Happened

1 Peter 2:24
By His stripes we were healed.

7 Sources of Life and Health

1. **The Word**
   Proverbs 3:1–2
   Proverbs 4:22
2. **Biblically Trained Elders**
   James 5:15
   Prayer of faith / Anointing oil
3. **Confessing Your Faults**
   James 5:16
4. **Words of Your Mouth**
   Proverbs 12:18

5. **Fasting**
   Isaiah 58:8
6. **Staying in Love With the Lord**
   Psalm 91:16
7. **Honor Mother and Father**
   Deuteronomy 5:16

JEHOVAH-RAPHA IS THE NAME OF OUR GOD

1. Exodus 15:26
   His very nature is to heal us.
2. James 5:15
   He will forgive us and raise us up.
3. Isaiah 53:4–6
   He paid the price.
4. 1 Peter 2:21–24
   He was seen doing it.
5. Acts 10:38
   He proved it was His ministry.
6. Mark 16:15–18
   He anointed us for it.
7. Hebrews 13:8
   He's still doing it today.

◀A Life of Obedience

There are many people who will read this chapter and exempt themselves from its content and meaning because they are either Christians who do not attend church, or they don't know Jesus at all. This is sad because the Lord exempts no one from His ways—not the saint, not the sinner.

For ages, humans have fought for independence and freedom from tyranny and oppression. Especially here in America, we declare that all men are created equal. Notice the word "equal" used here. I am in total agreement that all humans are created equal and that we should fight against all evil dictators and their horrible treatment of fellow humans. I also agree that we need to be free from slavery and unlawful imprisonment. However, this is not what the Bible refers to when it says we are bondservants to the Lord Jesus Christ. When we declare our independence from Jesus Christ and His biblical system for our lives, we are certainly troubling ourselves. We are not only alienating ourselves, but we are causing ourselves a world of trauma.

Submission to Jesus and His Word is actually an act of freedom. It is not an act of being under bondage and control. I hear rebellious Christians constantly saying that the rules of engagement for Christians are just a form of bondage to a controlling spirit. I have heard the same people say that submission to God's ways and practices is only religious legalism or "old school." These independent sons and daughters of God are only hurting themselves. Their declaration of liberty and freedom from God's ways and commands is simply binding them to their rebellion and the wicked one. What a deception!

For example, when we tithe (a biblical, New Testament practice), we are actually declaring our independence from the world's system (see my book, *The Real Truth About Tithing*). When we decide to be conformed to His image rather than the world, we are initiating our freedom from the bonds of the devil and the world's system. When we submit to God and His ways, we are actually severing our connections to the world, the flesh, and the devil.

Most of us have been raised in the world's system, which is actually a Babylonian system. It is unscriptural in every way and almost totally ungodly. It requires worshiping everything from idols to spirits to possessions (and yes, even humans). In fact, one of the most popular gods of the day is "self."

Submission to our God is not just a decision. It is not just a belief that one holds dear inside his soul. It is not just emotional. It is not just religious. It is all of the above and more. It takes conviction. It takes inner fortitude and a consuming love for Jesus that overrides everything else. It takes action! The Bible teaches us that we must be doers of the Word and not just hearers. We learn this from the story of the man who built his house on the rock and from the Apostle James. The Bible is filled with this challenge to all those who follow Jesus Christ. Take a moment and review each of the following.

THE MAN WHO BUILT HIS HOUSE ON THE SAND

Matthew 7:26-27

And every one that heareth these sayings of mine, and doeth them not, shall be likened unto a foolish man, which built his house upon the sand: And the rain descended, and the floods came, and the winds blew, and beat upon that house; and it fell: and great was the fall of it.

THE APOSTLE JAMES' CHALLENGE

James 1:21-25

Wherefore lay apart all filthiness and superfluity of naughtiness, and receive with meekness the engrafted word, which is able to save your souls. But be ye doers of the word, and not hearers only, deceiving your own selves. For if any be a hearer of the word, and not a doer, he is like unto a man beholding his natural face in a glass: For he beholdeth himself, and goeth his way, and straightway forgetteth what manner of man he was. But whoso looketh into the perfect law of liberty, and continueth therein, he being not a forgetful hearer, but a doer of the work, this man shall be blessed in his deed.

The happiest and most productive people I know are those people who have submitted themselves to the Lord Jesus Christ **and live His style of life**. When you trade your lifestyle for Jesus' lifestyle, you will never be sorry. His very way of life leads you away from the sinful way that is slowly killing you. It has now been confirmed that the world's way of life is treacherous and deadly. It is confirmed by a great variety of researchers and organizations that drinking alcohol kills people. Smoking kills people. Drugs kill people. The gang life and the life of crime kill people. The ones who don't actually die are harmed or maimed for life. They are daily bleeding, and their life is slipping away.

Those who live a life of sin (and I am including worldly Christians) pierce themselves through with many sorrows. They destroy all they have. Their very lifestyle decays and corrupts their marriage covenant, their children, their health—even their money will soon betray them. Crime and the criminal are almost always discovered and caught, and the Bible says that your sin will always find you out.

The very way of Christ leads us out of the way of the world. It leads us away from the very places where evil lurks to harm us. It leads us away from the practices that harm our lives. Why anyone wouldn't want to live the way of Christ is beyond me.

Why die when you can live? Why live in hellish conditions when you can have abundant life? Why live in terrible darkness when you can live in the light? Why live in inner turmoil when you can live in inner peace? Why stay bound to vices and strongholds when you can be bound to Jesus and live in liberty?

It seems like common sense to me that we should want a higher level and quality of life. Some people believe that Jesus and the Church are just part of a belief system or a religious addition to their own lifestyle. Some believe that the Church is another hobby or a duty in life. Not so. These and all other excuses and misconceptions lead men to despair, hopelessness, and great pain.

The longer I serve Jesus and live the way of the Bible, the more I realize that these great Holy Scriptures are not just for Sunday. They are not just for the purposes of making us good church members. They are for everyday life, and they work in every area of life. The more we stand on His Word for guidance, the better decisions we make. The better the decisions, the better the outcome. The better the outcome, the higher quality of life we enjoy.

I am purposely spending this much time explaining this so you can see the reasons for obeying the Word. Take a look at what happens when you obey, and then we will discover the perils of disobedience.

Obedience and submission are easy. Disobedience and rebellion are complicated and painful. Living right is clean and clear. Living in sin requires covert activities and stealth behavior.

Here are a few examples of obedience and submission:

1. Hebrews 13:17
   Submit and obey your godly leaders, and you will profit.
2. Malachi 3:10–12
   Tithe, and you are blessed and protected.
3. Malachi 3:11
   Tithe, and the devourer is rebuked by God. The devourer is whatever is devouring your life right now.
4. Ecclesiastes 11:2
   Give, and evil is repelled.
5. Ecclesiastes 11:2
   Giving is in direct connection with being able to repel the evil that lurks for you.

6. Galatians 6:7–9
   Corruption is avoided when your giving is scriptural.

7. Matthew 6:14
   Forgive, and you will be forgiven.

8. John 16:23
   Pray, and it will be heard.

9. Psalm 119:11
   Put God's Word in your heart, and you will not sin.

10. 1 Timothy 4:15
    Read and meditate in the verses, and you will prosper.

11. Mark 10:47
    Cry out to God in trouble, and He will intervene.

12. Psalm 1:1–4
    Walk in His counsel, and you will be blessed and prosper.

13. Proverbs 4:20–23
    Health and strength to your flesh.

Actually, I could go on and on because there are literally dozens and dozens of verses that show what happens for an obedient son or daughter.

But what about disobedience? Disobedience is a form of rebellion. Rebellion is the same as the sin of witchcraft. It has the same repercussions as witchcraft, and it is to be judged the same. What is witchcraft? A witch has no powers of her own. She is a medium. She must make a covenant with the evil powers in order for her tools to work. If you go to a witch, voodoo doctor, psychic, palm reader, etc., you submit not only to them but to the evil spirits that work with them. Your connection to the witch gives the evil spirits permission to function in your life. They will not only reveal things about you, but they will enter your life and try to cause these predictions to come to pass. Again, if you go to a witch, the evil spirits interpret it as your permission and invitation to function in your life.

1 Samuel 15:23

For rebellion is as the sin of witchcraft, and stubbornness is as iniquity and idolatry. Because thou hast rejected the word of the Lord, he hath also rejected thee from being king.

Rebellion is as the sin of witchcraft. It is just as bad as witchcraft. It invites evil spirits into your life, and they can breach your perimeters because you personally broke the hedge. It is bad because God views it as your denying His word or refusing to search it out and instead going to another voice or source for direction.

When you are in rebellion and you disobey, it is interpreted by the evil spirits as permission to attack your life. When you disobey, you are in the act of rebellion to God and His Word. When you are in rebellion at any level, you are accomplishing the same thing as going to the witch.

Listen to me closely now. When you rebel against God and His Word in any area, **you don't need the witch**. In fact, to the evil spirits, **your rebellion is the witch**. Your rebellion takes the place of the witch. This is why so many Christians (who love God) have so many weird attacks and troubles. Most of them don't know about this, so they continue on blindly and suffer the consequences.

A good example is tithing. I don't use this example because it relates to money but rather protection. When one does not tithe, they are telling God that they can handle this part of their life without His protection. You don't have to tithe. In fact, you don't **have to** do anything God says, BUT . . . if you don't, it will be very painful. It is considered rebellious. If you tithe, the devourer is rebuked on your behalf. If you don't, it isn't. The devourer is not always the devil himself. Many times it is simply whatever is devouring your life. Maybe it is depression or some disease. Perhaps it is chronic poverty or lack. There are many enemies that must be dealt with, or they will not go away. You cannot wish them away. You cannot want them to leave you alone yet continue to do and say those things that invite them into your life. This is simple "spiritual math."

So, when you do not tithe, Heaven interprets it as your denying God's help and that you are declaring your independence from God's system of protection and defense. You are interpreted by Heaven as saying that you need no help handling your devourer when it comes to strike you. I am not exaggerating this at all. Whether you can see and understand this spirit realm or not, it does exist and it is very active all around you.

This is so important to your well being that I am going to go over it again and again. The Bible promises us supernatural protection through God when we tithe. Malachi 3:8–12 tells us the devourer will actually be rebuked by God. When we don't tithe, we are telling Heaven that we are taking matters into our own hands. We are saying, "Thanks, but no thanks." We are saying, "I love You, Lord, but in this part of my life, I am on my own. I can do this without You."

If we don't tithe, the evil spirits interpret it as though we are telling God we don't need Him. To them, it means we are unprotected because we are choosing to turn down God's protection.

I am not a spooky person who thinks that every little turbulence or bump in the road is a demon that must be dealt with. However, I do know that demons are real, and they work hard to find an area of your life where they can wreak havoc. The more you can do to stop them, the higher quality of life you will live. No one is exempt from this. You can live in truth or error. You can live in power or weakness. You can live happily or always sad. You must learn this Bible and actually live by it every day. You must obey.

Matthew 19:17

And he said unto him, Why callest thou me good? there is none good but one, that is, God: but if thou wilt enter into life, keep the commandments.

John 14:15

If ye love me, keep my commandments.
[commandments, not suggestions]

John 14:21

He that hath my commandments, and keepeth them, he it is that loveth me: and he that loveth me shall be loved of my Father, and I will love him, and will manifest myself to him.

John 15:9–10

As the Father hath loved me, so have I loved you: continue ye in my love. If ye keep my commandments, ye shall abide in my love; even as I have kept my Father's commandments, and abide in his love.

One of the greatest deceptions of all times is self-deception. To hear His Word and not live it is to deceive oneself.

James 1:22-25

But be ye doers of the word, and not hearers only, deceiving your own selves. For if any be a hearer of the word, and not a doer, he is like unto a man beholding his natural face in a glass: For he beholdeth himself, and goeth his way, and straightway forgetteth what manner of man he was. But whoso looketh into the perfect law of liberty, and continueth therein, he being not a forgetful hearer, but a doer of the work, this man shall be blessed in his deed.

As I close this chapter, I'd like to challenge you to live in line with the Holy Scriptures. Even if you don't consider yourself to be a good Christian or a steady churchgoer, it will do no harm to read and meditate in the verses. You will do yourself a great service by it. Eventually you will be stronger and wiser and live a better life.

Since I met Jesus and invited Him into my heart, I have sought for His best. That's what I want for my family—the highest quality of life we can possibly have, the best health, the best finances, the greatest peace, the best family, the best of everything—His best. I want this for you also. The Lord wants this for you. This is the reason I wrote this and many other books.

◀A Spiritual Immune System

THE BUILT-IN SPIRITUAL IMMUNE SYSTEM

Your conscience is your spiritual immune system. Just like your physical immune system, the healthier it is, the more it attacks its enemies. Many people today fall prey to spiritual enemies because their conscience is all clogged up and sluggish. Many people cannot resist temptation and certainly cannot beat sin due to a sick or seared conscience.

If your conscience is defiled, it will not warn you sufficiently and especially not in a timely manner. If your conscience is sluggish, it will not produce conviction. If your conscience does not produce conviction, you will never feel sorry about the bad things you are doing. If you never feel sorry about the bad things you are doing, you will never feel led to quit doing them. If you don't quit the bad things you are doing, they will slowly corrupt you and finally destroy you.

We all have a built-in immune system. We have a physical immune system that helps us fight off bacteria and diseases so we can live a strong, healthy life. We also have a spiritual immune system over which our conscience is the master controller. As Christians, we have an opportunity to tweak our conscience and therefore keep it working at peak performance.

This is the gift of God to His children. It is our God-given privilege to be able to not only resist sin but conquer it.

In times past, many goodhearted preachers taught against sin because they were either religious or trying to get people to be religious. Without criticizing them, I want to tell you that my motive is different. Certainly I am for religion in its proper biblical definition, but I am totally against religiosity. There is a big difference between Christianity and man-made religious practices. I intend to improve your life and make you ferocious against your enemies by showing you how to fortify your spiritual immune system. What I am about to teach you will work not only in church but in your everyday life.

CONSCIENCE AND CONVICTION

Your conscience has two major functions in your life—to cause conviction or guilt. I sometimes compare it to the organ in your physical body called your pancreas. Its two major functions are to release the hormones glucagon or insulin into your bloodstream to maintain properly balanced levels. Without this help, your levels will either peak too high or fall to the bottom. It is mandatory for the pancreas to release these with great precision, both the timing and levels.

Your body just unwrapped that chocolate bar, and with the first bite your pancreas yells, "General quarters, general quarters, all hands, man your battle stations. This is not a drill, this is not a drill." It prepares for that sugar attack that is about to invade your system.

Your conscience is just that important to your well-being. As a matter of fact, it is crucial to your survival. Your conscience produces two major elements—one is conviction, and the other is guilt.

Conviction is important because it keeps us from committing evil. It can be a still, small voice or a roaring shout of warning. It is meant to activate while you are in the temptation stage. As sin tries its best to enter your life, your conscience kicks in with conviction. If a little bit of conviction will steer you away from the temptation, that is all you hear—that still, small voice. If you push past that still, small voice, your conscience releases even more conviction and starts to scream at you. It will do all it possibly can to stop you from sinning. That's its job.

The Word tells us about those who were convicted by their own conscience:

John 8:9

And they which heard it, being convicted by their own conscience, went out one by one, beginning at the eldest, even unto the last: and Jesus was left alone, and the woman standing in the midst.

Your conscience will also produce conviction to drive you to do what is right. This powerful inner friend is the motivator that tells you to get off the couch and get to church. It will convict you to read your Bible, present your tithe, and forgive your brother. It is clear that we need this life-adjusting conviction, both to warn us to stay out of sin and to drive us to make the right decisions. I have known many people who push past conviction and practice sin anyway.

CONSCIENCE AND GUILT

Your conscience has another purpose. It has the duty to produce guilt when you push past the conviction and sin anyway. That's right, guilt. Don't confuse this with condemnation. True guilt is that feeling of disappointing God, that feeling of doing wrong and feeling badly about your wrongdoing. If we never had guilt (or godly sorrow), we would never feel the need to repent.

2 Corinthians 7:10

For godly sorrow worketh repentance to salvation not to be repented of: but the sorrow of the world worketh death.

It is not good to sin. It is not only displeasing to God, but it robs us something fierce. Sin will steal all your increase.

Job 31:12

For it is a fire that consumeth to destruction, and would root out all mine increase.

Of course we all know that death is sin's wage.

Romans 6:23

For the wages of sin is death; but the gift of God is eternal life through Jesus Christ our Lord.

If you sin against your wife, you will "kill" your marriage. Even if she keeps you, you will "kill" the confidence that she had in you. If you sin against your boss, you will "kill" your job. If you sin against your boss severely enough, you will "kill" your future employment opportunities, etc.

When we do sin, our conscience kicks in and produces a special guilt. This guilt, known as godly sorrow, teaches us and convinces us to repent. Repentance is the God-given system for reconciliation. When we push past conviction and sin anyway, guilt says to stop now and turn away. It dictates that we turn back to God and ask Him for forgiveness.

Now remember that if guilt goes sour, it will turn into condemnation. This is not of God. Condemnation is that ugly feeling that condemns you for what you did or are doing and then belittles you for doing it. It blocks your freedom and deliverance. It keeps you in your sin, and it gives you a distorted sin consciousness.

CONSCIENCE VOID OF OFFENSE TOWARD GOD

A conscience should be void of all offense toward God.

Acts 24:16
And herein do I exercise myself, to have always a conscience void of offence toward God, and toward men.

A healthy conscience is the well of life. It is your guarantee to freedom and dominion. This is by far not automatic; neither does it develop by itself. It does not matter how long you have been a Christian. You must work at this in order to have a spiritually healthy conscience.

A conscience that is void or empty of offense toward God is a conscience that has been cleansed and is free from ungodly elements. Ungodly elements include a very long list of things that are repulsive to Jesus, your Savior. Among them are unforgiveness, prejudice, pornography, sexual lust, gossip, and anger.

A conscience void of offense toward men is a conscience that holds no grudges and does not try to get even. It is a conscience that does not covet anything belonging to his neighbor and never schemes to hurt or destroy another. It is a conscience that does not think evil of anyone.

A WEAK CONSCIENCE WILL BECOME DEFILED

The following verse shows us that some have a weak conscience, and therefore their conscience is defiled.

1 Corinthians 8:7

Howbeit there is not in every man that knowledge: for some with conscience of the idol unto this hour eat it as a thing offered unto an idol; and their conscience being weak is defiled.

This scripture proves that a weak conscience will permit things to remain in your life that bring offense toward God. A weak conscience will not be able to stop you from sinning. It's not so much that a weak conscience permits you to sin but that is doesn't possess the strength to convince you differently.

The defiled have a defiled conscience and a defiled mind. This actually aids in causing them to be defiled. Again, if you allow your conscience to become weak and then defiled, you will slowly begin to live a defiled life and eventually self-destruct.

We have many verses that tell us to renew our mind and be transformed. As a new convert comes into this great Kingdom of ours, they must have their mind washed with the water of the Word of God. "That he might sanctify and cleanse it with the washing of water by the word" (Eph. 5:26). They must be transformed by the renewing of their mind.

Romans 12:1-2

I beseech you therefore, brethren, by the mercies of God, that ye present your bodies a living sacrifice, holy, acceptable unto God, which is your reasonable service. And be not conformed to this world: but be ye transformed by the renewing of your mind, that ye may prove what is that good, and acceptable, and perfect, will of God.

Titus 1:15

Unto the pure all things are pure: but unto them that are defiled and unbelieving is nothing pure; but even their mind and conscience is defiled.

A CONSCIENCE SEARED WITH A HOT IRON

Having their conscience seared with a hot iron . . .

1 Timothy 4:2

Speaking lies in hypocrisy; having their conscience seared with a hot iron . . .

Sin does this to you. It makes you dull of hearing and hardened to the still, small voice within. It will sear your conscience so that it cannot do its job. If your conscience is seared, it will not be able to accurately produce enough conviction quickly enough to keep you out of sin. If your conscience is seared, it will not produce enough conviction to motivate you to do even the basic practices of Christianity. If your conscience is seared, it will not produce enough guilt (godly sorrow), and therefore you will not repent and turn away from your sins. If you don't repent and turn away from your sins, you will face every day with unconfessed, open sin in your life. This is a formula for disaster!

Check out this verse:

Hebrews 10:26

For if we sin willfully after that we have received the knowledge of the truth, there remaineth no more sacrifice for sins.

This is the problem, my friend. This is a formula for disaster, satan's strike, and self-destruction. Our sins are only forgiven if we confess them. "If we confess our sins, he is faithful and just to forgive us our sins, and to cleanse us from all unrighteousness" (1 John 1:9).

What if your conscience is seared and you don't confess your sins? Here's how it works. When you sin, it is because you pushed past the conviction that your conscience produced to warn you and stop you. Every time you ignore this inner voice of conviction, you sear your conscience a little. As you get used to sinning and denying conviction, you sear your conscience even more. As time goes by, your conscience is so seared, you are no longer sensitive to its convicting power.

You will sin without conviction, and you will cast off all restraint. Your life then becomes defiled. You then begin defiling others around you, and your actions and decisions are defiled. Trouble has really set in by this time.

The same is true with guilt. (Remember, guilt is not condemnation.) When your conscience is seared from sinning often, you will eventually stop repenting and asking for forgiveness. Now you are really in trouble—big trouble.

IGNORE YOUR CONSCIENCE, YOU GO SHIPWRECK

1 Timothy 1:5
Now the end of the commandment is charity out of a pure heart, and of a good conscience, and of faith unfeigned...

1 Timothy 1:19
Holding faith, and a good conscience; which some having put away concerning faith have made shipwreck...

It is simple, actually. If you do not pay attention to your conscience, you will end up going shipwreck in the faith and in life. I know people who have done this. I suppose I will know many more by the time this life is over. If you hold to your good conscience, you will follow the conviction to do what is right, and you will deny sin.

Let's remember that God gave us this conscience to make us pure and keep us pure. Purity allows us to see the Lord. It gives us a pure heart and clean hands.

Psalm 24:3-5

Who shall ascend into the hill of the LORD? or who shall stand in his holy place? He that hath clean hands, and a pure heart; who hath not lifted up his soul unto vanity, nor sworn deceitfully. He shall receive the blessing from the LORD, and righteousness from the God of his salvation.

Even if you push past the conscience-produced conviction, you can at least fall back on the conscience-produced guilt that will convince you to repent and get back to God's way.

I want to bring your attention back to 1 Timothy 1:19 and the Word of God that teaches us to never set aside our faith or our good conscience. Do not ignore or deny your conscience when it speaks to you. Learn to listen to it, and your life will be blessed. There is much more to say about this subject, but I suppose it's for another time.

Before we close out this chapter, let's take a brief look at how we can keep our conscience strong and healthy. How can we build up this spiritual immune system?

HOW TO HAVE A CLEAN, HEALTHY CONSCIENCE

As Christians who walk closely with God, we have learned many good ways to keep ourselves clean and untainted from such a filthy and evil world. As you endeavor to walk this closely with Jesus, you will also learn some things on your own. For now, however, here are a few hints to get you started.

Wash your mind constantly.

Ephesians 5:26

That he might sanctify and cleanse it with the washing of water by the word . . .

Renew your mind consistently.

Romans 12:2

And be not conformed to this world: but be ye transformed by the renewing of your mind, that ye may prove what is that good, and acceptable, and perfect, will of God.

Purge and cleanse yourself.

2 Timothy 2:21

If a man therefore purge himself from these, he shall be a vessel unto honour, sanctified, and meet for the master's use, and prepared unto every good work.

Forgive everyone for everything—NOW!

Matthew 18:21–22

Then came Peter to him, and said, Lord, how oft shall my brother sin against me, and I forgive him? till seven times? Jesus saith unto him, I say not unto thee, Until seven times: but, Until seventy times seven.

Memorize and meditate upon His Word.

Psalm 119:11

Thy word have I hid in mine heart, that I might not sin against thee.

Repent of everything; ask God and others to forgive you.

Acts 3:19

Repent ye therefore, and be converted, that your sins may be blotted out, when the times of refreshing shall come from the presence of the Lord . . .

Give great attention to even small matters that may quench the Holy Spirit.

1 Thessalonians 5:19

Quench not the Spirit.

Ephesians 4:30

And grieve not the holy Spirit of God, whereby ye are sealed unto the day of redemption.

Think on these things . . .

Philippians 4:8

Finally, brethren, whatsoever things are true, whatsoever things are honest, whatsoever things are just, whatsoever things are pure, whatsoever things are lovely, whatsoever things are of good report; if there be any virtue, and if there be any praise, think on these things.

Cleanse your environment—your eyes and ears are your largest junk collectors.

2 Corinthians 7:1

Having therefore these promises, dearly beloved, let us cleanse ourselves from all filthiness of the flesh and spirit, perfecting holiness in the fear of God.

Fill your soul with God's music—not that of the world, the flesh, and the devil.

1 Samuel 16:23

. . . David took an harp, and played with his hand: so Saul was refreshed, and was well, and the evil spirit departed from him.

Avoid sin like the plague that it is.

Romans 13:14

But put ye on the Lord Jesus Christ, and make not provision for the flesh, to fulfil the lusts thereof.

Avoid the very appearance of sin.

1 Thessalonians 5:22

Abstain from all appearance of evil.

If you are concerned about how something "looks" to others, you will certainly not proceed.

A GREAT QUOTE FROM A GREAT MAN

Two natures beat within my breast.
One is cursed, and one is blessed.
One I love, and one I hate.
The one I feed will dominate.

—Dr. Roy Hicks Sr.

Chapter 11

igns of the End

The Bible is very clear about what we are to look for during the last days. There are many different warnings and insights about which the preachers and prophets of old foretold us. I will list a few of them, but realize there are many more than I have included in this book.

When we look at the writings of Jesus Christ, the apostles, and the prophets, we clearly see a picture of the last of the last days. There are many eye-opening and eyebrow-raising verses. This is what we are to expect, and this is what is happening and will happen all around us as the end comes near.

These verses are the key to our future, a light to our path. We must not ignore them. We must not treat them lightly. We must not deny them. We must obey and pay attention to them. We must take them to heart, and we must force our lifestyle to line up to their standard.

JESUS' WARNINGS

The Day of Noah

Matthew 24:37

But as the days of Noe were, so shall also the coming of the Son of man be.

Matthew 24:38

For as in the days that were before the flood they were eating and drinking, marrying and giving in marriage, until the day that Noe entered into the ark ...

Luke 17:26

And as it was in the days of Noe, so shall it be also in the days of the Son of man.

Luke 17:27

They did eat, they drank, they married wives, they were given in marriage, until the day that Noe entered into the ark, and the flood came, and destroyed them all.

In other words, people were living their lives as if there were no end coming and no danger around them. They mocked Noah and his family and thought they were very weird and too religious—that is, until the judgment came. Then they converted quickly, and all wanted a place on the ark. Too late!

It was the same in Lot's day.

The Day of Lot

Luke 17:28

Likewise also as it was in the days of Lot; they did eat, they drank, they bought, they sold, they planted, they builded ...

Luke 17:29

But the same day that Lot went out of Sodom it rained fire and brimstone from heaven, and destroyed them all.

Weather Patterns and Wars

Matthew 24:7

For nation shall rise against nation, and kingdom against kingdom: and there shall be famines, and pestilences, and earthquakes, in divers places.

Mark 13:8

For nation shall rise against nation, and kingdom against kingdom: and there shall be earthquakes in divers places, and there shall be famines and troubles: these are the beginnings of sorrows.

Luke 21:11

And great earthquakes shall be in divers places, and famines, and pestilences; and fearful sights and great signs shall there be from heaven.

Deception

Matthew 24:4

And Jesus answered and said unto them, Take heed that no man deceive you.

Matthew 24:5

For many shall come in my name, saying, I am Christ; and shall deceive many.

Matthew 24:11

And many false prophets shall rise, and shall deceive many.

Matthew 24:24

For there shall arise false Christs, and false prophets, and shall shew great signs and wonders; insomuch that, if it were possible, they shall deceive the very elect.

Mark 13:5

And Jesus answering them began to say, Take heed lest any man deceive you . . .

Mark 13:6

For many shall come in my name, saying, I am Christ; and shall deceive many.

Let's make a list of the things about which Jesus warned us:

1. Feasting, partying, marrying
2. Ignoring the times and warnings until judgment fell
3. Buying, selling, planting, and building (This reminds me of the up-and-down stock market frenzy to buy one day and sell the next. It also reminds me of the Babylonian system and people who ignore the times and push forward by borrowing.)
4. Ethnic groups rising against each other
5. Kingdoms rising against each other
6. Famines
7. Earthquakes in different places (causing tsunamis)
8. Great earthquakes
9. Troubled weather patterns, hurricanes, tornadoes, floods, etc.
10. Pestilences
11. Fearful sights
12. Great deception from men

13. Many calling themselves "the anointed one"
14. False prophets
15. False signs and wonders
16. False teachers
17. False doctrines

PAUL

Everyone concedes to the fact that Jesus Christ Himself appointed the Apostle Paul as the first apostle to the Gentiles. Not only did he have Heaven's experience but also Heaven's guidance, revelation, and impartations. This great apostle was given the assignment of establishing the Gentile Church and laying its foundation. Paul had a great insight about these last days. He absolutely had a revelation about what was coming and how things would be for the future of the Church.

Let's take a closer look:

Departing From the Faith

1 Timothy 4:1

Now the Spirit speaketh expressly, that in the latter times some shall depart from the faith, giving heed to seducing spirits, and doctrines of devils . . .

A Falling Away

2 Thessalonians 2:3

Let no man deceive you by any means: for that day shall not come, except there come a falling away first, and that man of sin be revealed, the son of perdition . . .

Perilous Times

2 Timothy 3:1

This know also, that in the last days perilous times shall come.

2 Timothy 3:2

For men shall be lovers of their own selves, covetous, boasters, proud, blasphemers, disobedient to parents, unthankful, unholy . . .

2 Timothy 3:3

Without natural affection, trucebreakers, false accusers, incontinent, fierce, despisers of those that are good . . .

2 Timothy 3:4

Traitors, heady, highminded, lovers of pleasures more than lovers of God . . .

2 Timothy 3:5

Having a form of godliness, but denying the power thereof: from such turn away.

2 Timothy 3:6

For of this sort are they which creep into houses, and lead captive silly women laden with sins, led away with divers lusts . . .

2 Timothy 3:7

Ever learning, and never able to come to the knowledge of the truth.

2 Timothy 3:8

Now as Jannes and Jambres withstood Moses, so do these also resist the truth: men of corrupt minds, reprobate concerning the faith.

2 Timothy 3:9

But they shall proceed no further: for their folly shall be manifest unto all men, as their's also was.

Humans Dangerously Misbehaving

Let's take a closer look at what Paul saw concerning people. Obviously this entire chapter is mostly about Christians and their deterioration. You are living on the earth today, so these things are not news to you. Even so, they bring understanding about why people are misbehaving and hurting each other.

Men shall be . . .

2 Timothy 3:2

1. Lovers of their own selves
2. Covetous
3. Boasters
4. Proud
5. Blasphemers
6. Disobedient to parents

7. Unthankful
8. Unholy

   2 Timothy 3:3

9. Without natural affection
10. Trucebreakers
11. False accusers
12. Incontinent
13. Fierce
14. Despisers of those that are good

   2 Timothy 3:4

15. Traitors
16. Heady
17. Highminded
18. Lovers of pleasures more than lovers of God

   2 Timothy 3:5

19. Having a form of godliness, but denying the power thereof

   2 Timothy 3:6

20. They creep into houses, and lead captive silly women laden with sins, led away with divers lusts.

   2 Timothy 3:7

21. Ever learning, and never able to come to the knowledge of the truth

2 Timothy 3:8

22. These also resist the truth.
23. Men of corrupt minds
24. Reprobate concerning the faith

2 Timothy 3:9

25. They shall proceed no further.
26. Their folly shall be manifest unto all men.

Will Not Endure Sound Doctrine

2 Timothy 4:3

For the time will come when they will not endure sound doctrine; but after their own lusts shall they heap to themselves teachers, having itching ears . . .

2 Timothy 4:4

And they shall turn away their ears from the truth, and shall be turned unto fables.

Let's continue our list:

27. Not endure (put up with) sound doctrine
28. Find teachers that give them what they want to hear
29. Turn away their ears from the truth
30. Turned unto fables

JOHN

Antichrists

1 John 2:18

Little children, it is the last time: and as ye have heard that antichrist shall come, even now are there many antichrists; whereby we know that it is the last time.

Dirty Garments

Revelation 3:4

Thou hast a few names even in Sardis which have not defiled their garments; and they shall walk with me in white: for they are worthy.

Lukewarm, Bragging Christians

Revelation 3:14

And unto the angel of the church of the Laodiceans write; These things saith the Amen, the faithful and true witness, the beginning of the creation of God . . .

Revelation 3:15

I know thy works, that thou art neither cold nor hot: I would thou wert cold or hot.

Revelation 3:16

So then because thou art lukewarm, and neither cold nor hot, I will spue thee out of my mouth.

Revelation 3:17

Because thou sayest, I am rich, and increased with goods, and have need of nothing; and knowest not that thou art wretched, and miserable, and poor, and blind, and naked . . .

The Nicolaitanes

Mixing the pagan practices of the sinner with the sacred practices of the Christian.

Revelation 2:6

But this thou hast, that thou hatest the deeds of the Nicolaitanes, which I also hate.

Revelation 2:15

So hast thou also them that hold the doctrine of the Nicolaitanes, which thing I hate.

Here is John's list of last-days happenings. Remember, this is not inclusive of everything he wrote or saw:

1. People behaving under the power of antichrist spirits
2. Christians dirtying their garments (lifestyle)
3. Lukewarm, bragging Christians
4. People acting like Nicolaitanes and mixing the dirty with the clean
5. People mixing false doctrines with truth
6. People claiming to be Christians but living like sinners

PETER

Scoffers

2 Peter 3:3

Knowing this first, that there shall come in the last days scoffers, walking after their own lusts ...

ISAIAH

The Lord's House

Isaiah 2:2

And it shall come to pass in the last days, that the mountain of the LORD'S house shall be established in the top of the mountains, and shall be exalted above the hills; and all nations shall flow unto it.

Isaiah 2:3

And many people shall go and say, Come ye, and let us go up to the mountain of the LORD, to the house of the God of Jacob; and he will teach us of his ways, and we will walk in his paths: for out of Zion shall go forth the law, and the word of the LORD from Jerusalem.

MICAH

One of the signs of the last days is the condition and elevation of God's House. That's right, God's House. Isaiah told us that "many" people will attend church in the last days. The Prophet Micah prophesied about this.

The Lord's House Popular

Micah 4:1

But in the last days it shall come to pass, that the mountain of the house of the LORD shall be established in the top of the mountains, and it shall be exalted above the hills; and people shall flow unto it.

Micah 4:2

And many nations shall come, and say, Come, and let us go up to the mountain of the LORD, and to the house of the God of Jacob; and he will teach us of his ways, and we will walk in his paths: for the law shall go forth of Zion, and the word of the LORD from Jerusalem.

CALLING EVIL GOOD AND GOOD EVIL

Isaiah 5:20

Woe unto them that call evil good, and good evil; that put darkness for light, and light for darkness; that put bitter for sweet, and sweet for bitter!

Isaiah 5:21

Woe unto them that are wise in their own eyes, and prudent in their own sight!

Isaiah 5:22

Woe unto them that are mighty to drink wine, and men of strength to mingle strong drink . . .

Isaiah 5:23

Which justify the wicked for reward, and take away the righteousness of the righteous from him!

Amos 5:14

Seek good, and not evil, that ye may live: and so the LORD, the God of hosts, shall be with you, as ye have spoken.

Amos 5:14

Hate the evil, and love the good, and establish judgment in the gate: it may be that the LORD God of hosts will be gracious unto the remnant of Joseph.

MEETING THE LORD IN THE AIR

1 Thessalonians 4:13–18

But I would not have you to be ignorant, brethren, concerning them which are asleep, that ye sorrow not, even as others which have no hope. For if we believe that Jesus died and rose again, even so them also which sleep in Jesus will God bring with him. For this we say unto you by the word of the Lord, that we which are alive and remain unto the coming of the Lord shall not prevent them which are asleep. For the Lord himself shall descend from heaven with a shout, with the voice of the archangel, and with the trump of God: and the dead in Christ shall rise first: Then we which are alive and remain shall be caught up together with them in the clouds, to meet the Lord in the air: and so shall we ever be with the Lord. Wherefore comfort one another with these words.

Conclusion

My prayers are with you. I want you to know that all of us here at Mark Barclay Ministries are standing with you and believing with you for a successful walk throughout these last days. You can do it. You should do it. You should force yourself to live what the Bible says. You owe it to your family. You owe it to the Lord Jesus. You owe it to yourself.

The devil is counting on a pattern of old—that you will treat these warnings lightly and live every day doing your own thing. He is hoping you will be like so many others before you and follow your lusts and desires instead of the Lord's wishes for you.

I highly recommend that you examine yourself and make every little adjustment possible to line up to the Word of God. We must be in the will of God and under His divine leadership and protective covering. We must prepare ourselves for the many who will fall, the many who will walk away from the way of the Lord, and the many who will be consumed by the filth of the day and the dangers lurking in the shadows.

We are already seeing many of these things come to pass. We are, right now, in the last of the last days—the climax of the ages—witnessing the self-destruction of many. We are witnessing the fulfillment of biblical prophetic utterances. We are surrounded with the facts—the manifestations of the predictions of the end of all times.

Please don't treat this like it is everyday stuff. The human race has never been here before. It won't last long. Take full advantage of the Word of God, and get your life right with God.

I did my best (in writing this book) to inform you about the most important protections against the effects of the last days. If you will honestly, humbly, and with tenacity do these things, you will make it. You will see the Lord and come out favorably on Judgment Day.

If you don't know Jesus as your personal Lord and Savior, you must accept Him now. Ask Him into your heart, and confess Him as Lord and Savior. Call a Christian friend, and let them know what you just did. They will help you prepare for your future. If you don't know whom to contact, please call upon us at Mark Barclay Ministries. You will not be able to make it by yourself.

If you have cooled off or backslidden, return home to your church as fast as possible. You cannot wait any longer. The time is too short. Do not get caught like a thief in the night. You must act now. Do not allow the filth and deceiving spirits of the day to drag you away to a dirty lifestyle and eventually to hell.

As you have discovered, this is a short, fast-reading book and one that you should keep close by and read through from time-to-time.

Job 17:9

The righteous also shall hold on his way, and he that hath clean hands shall be stronger and stronger.

Acts 3:19

Repent ye therefore, and be converted, that your sins may be blotted out, when the times of refreshing shall come from the presence of the Lord.

Luke 21:36

Watch ye therefore, and pray always, that ye may be accounted worthy to escape all these things that shall come to pass, and to stand before the Son of man.

Be sure to check out other books I have written and our Web site at www.marktbarclay.com. I am looking forward to meeting you in Heaven!

A Prayer of Salvation

YOU CAN BE SAVED
FROM ETERNAL DAMNATION!

Get God's help now, in this life. All you have to do is humble your heart, believe in Christ's work at Calvary for you, and pray the following prayer:

Dear Heavenly Father,

I know that I have sinned and fallen short of Your expectations of me. I have come to realize that I cannot run my own life. I do not want to continue the way I've been living, neither do I want to face an eternity of torment and damnation.

I know that the wages of sin is death, but I can be spared from this through the gift of the Lord Jesus Christ. I believe that He died for me, and I receive His provision now. I will not be ashamed of Him, and I will tell all my friends and family members that I have made this wonderful decision.

Dear Lord Jesus,

Come into my heart now and live in me and be my Savior, Master, and Lord. I will do my very best to chase after You and to learn Your ways by submitting to a pastor, reading my Bible, going to a church that preaches about You, and keeping sin out of my life.

I also ask You to give me the power to be healed from all sickness and disease and to deliver me from those things that have me bound.

I love You and thank You for having me, and I am eagerly looking forward to a long, beautiful relationship with You.

OTHER MATERIALS
BY MARK T. BARCLAY

BOOKS

Avoiding the Pitfalls of Familiarity
This book is a scriptural study about the most devastating sin in the body of Christ today. The truths in this book will make you aware of this excess familiarity and reveal to you some counterattacks.

Beware of Seducing Spirits
This is not a book on demonology. It is a book about people who are close to being in trouble with God because of demonic activity or fleshly bad attitudes.

Building a Supernatural Church
A step-by-step guide to pioneering, organizing, and establishing a local church.

Enduring Hardness
God has designed a program for His saints that will cause each one to be enlarged and victorious. This book will challenge your stability, steadfastness, courage, endurance, and determination and will motivate you to become a fighter.

How to Always Reap a Harvest
In this book, Dr. Barclay explains the principles that help us to be successful and fruitful. It explains how to live a better life, become far more productive, and enjoy a full harvest.

How to Avoid Shipwreck
A book of preventives, helping people to remain strong and full of faith. You will be strengthened by this book as you learn how to anchor your soul.

How to Relate to Your Pastor
It is very important in these last days that God's people understand the office of pastor. As we put into practice these principles, the Church will grow in numbers and also increase its vision for the world.

How to Survive a Betrayal
Often the most difficult thing to deal with concerning betrayal is the fact that it almost always comes from the people you love, trust, or respect. This amazing book will help you press on, recover, and once again become productive when a betrayal strikes your heart.

Improving Your Performance
Every leader everywhere needs to read this book. It will help tremendously in the organization and unity of your ministry and work force.

Preachers of Righteousness
As you read this book, you will be both edified and challenged to not only do the work of the ministry but to do it with humility, honesty, and godliness.

The Real Truth About Tithing
With the extremely fast-paced lifestyle of these last days, it leaves little time to thoroughly study God's Word. When you finish this book, you will be fully equipped and informed to tithe properly and accurately. All of your tithing questions should be answered. Your life will never be the same.

Sheep, Goats, and Wolves
A scriptural yet practical explanation of human behavior in our local churches and how church leaders and members can deal with each other.

Six Ways to Check Your Leadings

It seems that staying in the main flow of Jesus is one of the most difficult things for believers to do, including some preachers. Many people border on mysticism and a world of fantasy. God is not a goofy god. He doesn't intend for His people to be goofy either. This book reveals the six most valuable New Testament ways to live in accuracy and stay perfectly on course. This book is a must for living in these last days.

The Making of a Man of God

In this book you'll find some of the greatest yet simplest insights to becoming a man or woman of God and launching your ministry with accuracy and credibility. The longevity of your ministry will be enhanced by these truths.

The Sin of Lawlessness

Lawlessness always challenges authority and ultimately is designed to hurt people. This book will convict those who are in lawlessness and warn those who could be future victims. It will help your life and straighten your walk with Him.

The Remnant

God has always had a people and will always have a people. Dr. Barclay speaks of the upcoming revival and how we can be those who are alive and remain when our Master returns.

Walking With God

A handbook for the Spirit-filled life, this book is sure to stir you on in pursuing more of the things of the Spirit. It also makes a great gift for those who don't understand the Spirit-filled life, giving thorough explanation, mixed with real experience, regarding the following topics: The Ministry of the Holy Spirit; The Holy Spirit in Action; No Mere Man; Holy Spirit Baptism; The Anointing; Led by the

Spirit; How to Check Your Leadings; The Eyes of Your
Spirit; The Armor of God; The Fruit of the Spirit; The Gifts
of God; How to Develop in the Gifts; On Fire for God;
Making the Holy Spirit Your Best Friend!

Warring Mental Warfare
Every person is made up of body, soul, and spirit and
fights battles on each of these three fronts. The war
against your soul (made up of your mind, will, and emo-
tions) is real and as lethal as spiritual and natural enemies. This book will help you identify, war against, and
defeat the enemies of your soul. Learn to quit coping with
depression, anxiety, fear, and other hurts, and begin conquering those things now!

What About Death?
In this book, Brother Barclay deals with the enemy
(death) and how to overcome it. He also explains what
the Bible says about life after death. Many people have no
real Bible knowledge on this subject and therefore are
unsure about it all the days of their lives.

MINIBOOKS

Basic Christian Handbook
This book contains basic doctrines that are simple yet
necessary to every Christian's walk with God. It will be a
vital help to new converts in the Kingdom.

Have You Seen This Person Lately?
Did you once serve the Lord actively and fervently, but
now you have cooled off? Are you now serving Him and
want to assure that you will never backslide? Do you have
family or friends who are backslidden or unchurched?
Then this book is for you! Its contents will help you or
someone you care about find the way home.

The Captain's Mantle
Something happened in the cave Adullum. Find out how 400 distressed, indebted, and discontented men came out of that cave as one of the most awesome armies in history!

MANUALS

Ministry of Helps
The Ministry of Helps manual is a companion manual to the Minister's Manual and was written to help pastors, ministers, administrators, and other leaders to establish a strong and effective ministry of helps in the local church. Topics include training and qualifications, organization, communications, church leadership, having church, and more.

Minister's Manual
The Minister's Manual is a companion manual to the Ministry of Helps manual and was written with the specific needs of ministers in mind. Topics include ethics, governments, administration, building a ministry of helps, the local church, sacraments, pastoring the local church, executives, protocol, the supernatural and the practical, and more.

SERIES

How to Study Your Bible (CD or DVD)
In this powerful series, Brother Barclay offers three teachings on this vital topic. The first two titles cover how to study your Bible personally and at church. The third message offers insight into tools to help you study your Bible.

SUPERNATURAL MINISTRIES TRAINING INSTITUTE (SMTI)

"Building Believers for Ministry"

SMTI is a contemporary ministry training institute, specializing in spiritual Bible training—building, developing, and equipping believers with the Scriptures to function supernaturally in all areas of ministry. SMTI presents the uncompromised, practical, life-adjusting Word of God in a straightforward, understandable format that is applicable for a wide range of individuals (lay people as well as full-time ministers). SMTI designs and presents scriptural curriculum in a way that builds character, imparts vision, and provides insight about the end times—causing believers and churches to flourish and courageously climax the ages.

Curriculum

The SMTI curriculum includes three different courses of study. Each course is designed to be completed in a nine-month period (31 weeks of teachings). All classes are taught by Mark T. Barclay.

Supernatural Helps

Supernatural Helps is designed to build character, help define and perfect the call on an individual's life, and develop supportive ministries in the local church.

Ministerial Practicalities

Ministerial Practicalities will provide practical training about the local church, administration, legalities, ceremonies, executive ethics, and wisdom to perform with excellence in the ministry.

Advanced Survival Techniques

Advanced Survival Techniques is designed to help the end-time leaders and believers in dealing with the crucial matters of life and ministry.